THOR

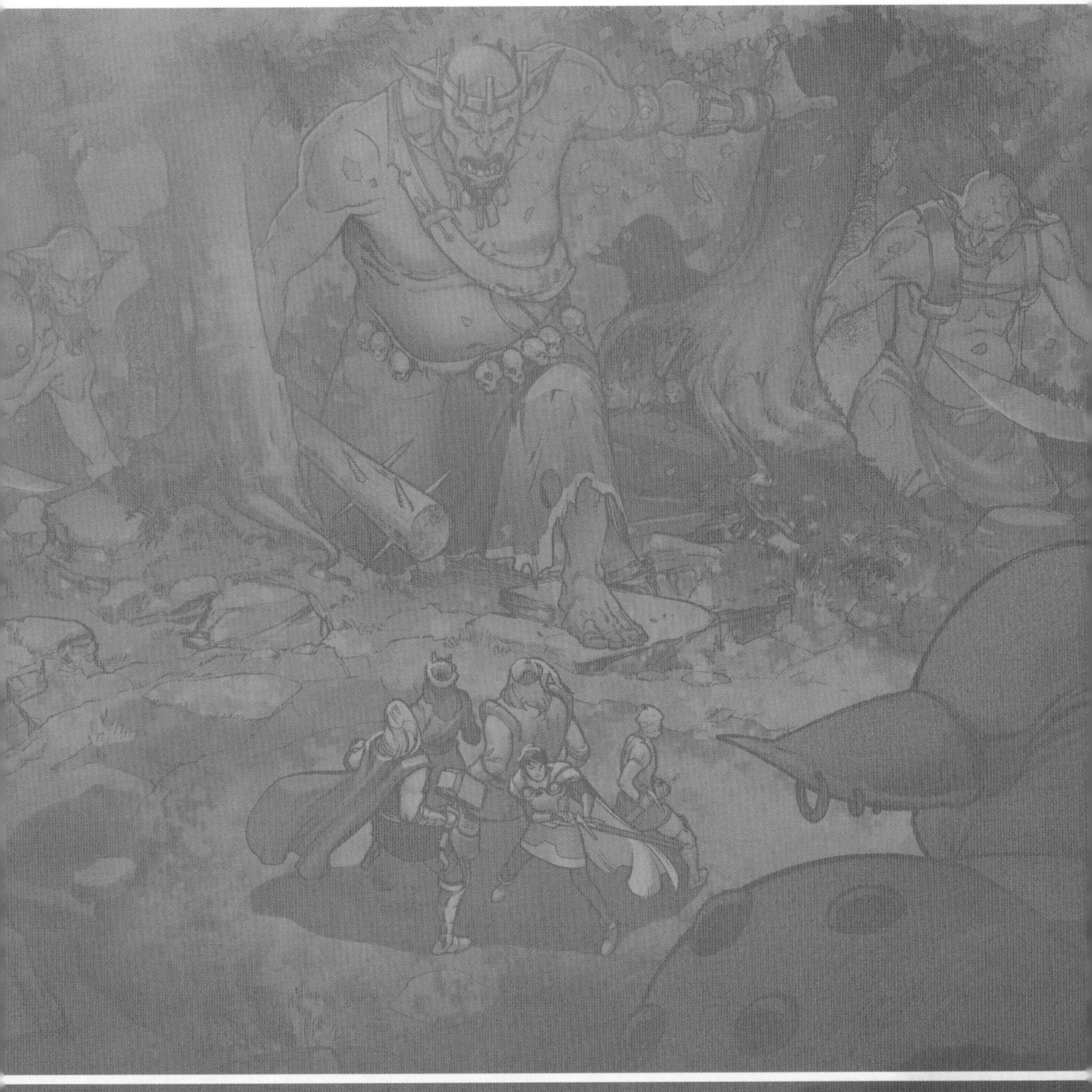

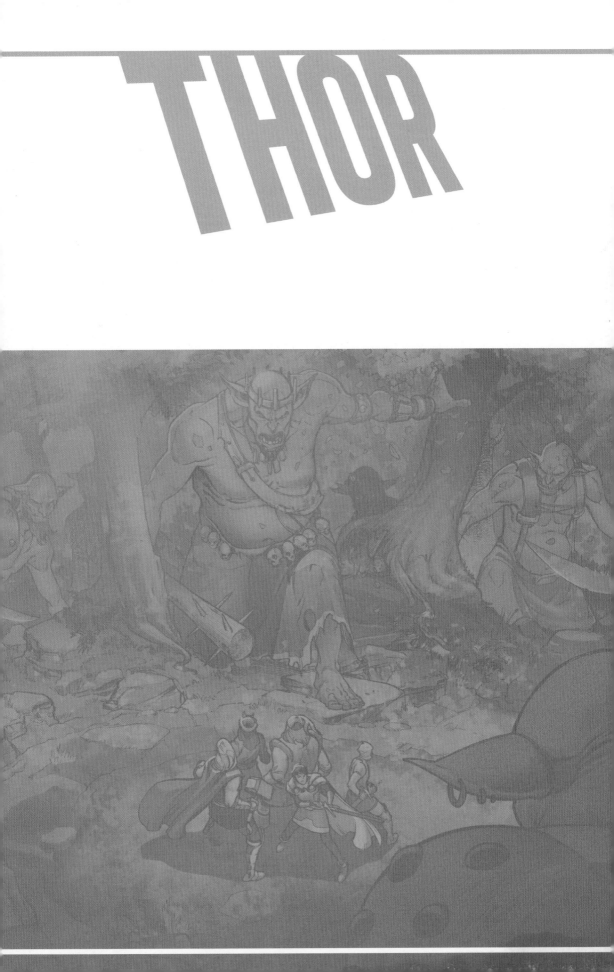

COLLECTION EDITOR: **JENNIFER GRÜNWALD**
ASSISTANT EDITORS: **ALEX STARBUCK & NELSON RIBEIRO**
EDITOR, SPECIAL PROJECTS: **MARK D. BEAZLEY**
SENIOR EDITOR, SPECIAL PROJECTS: **JEFF YOUNGQUIST**
SVP OF PRINT AND DIGITAL PUBLISHING SALES: **DAVID GABRIEL**
COVER & BOOK DESIGN: **JEFF POWELL**

EDITOR IN CHIEF: **AXEL ALONSO**
CHIEF CREATIVE OFFICER: **JOE QUESADA**
PUBLISHER: **DAN BUCKLEY**
EXECUTIVE PRODUCER: **ALAN FINE**

THOR: SEASON ONE. Contains material originally published in magazine form as THOR: GOD OF THUNDER #1. First printing 2013. ISBN# 978-0-7851-5379-5. Published by MARVEL WORLDWIDE, INC., a subsidiary MARVEL ENTERTAINMENT, LLC. OFFICE OF PUBLICATION: 135 West 50th Street, New York, NY 10020. **Printed in the U.S.A.** ALAN FINE, EVP - Office of the President, Marvel Worldwide, Inc. and EVP & CMO Marv Characters B.V.; DAN BUCKLEY, Publisher & President - Print, Animation & Digital Divisions; JOE QUESADA, Chief Creative Officer; TOM BREVOORT, SVP of Publishing; DAVID BOGART, SVP of Operations & Procuremen Publishing; C.B. CEBULSKI, SVP of Creator & Content Development; DAVID GABRIEL, SVP of Print & Digital Publishing Sales; JIM O'KEEFE, VP of Operations & Logistics; DAN CARR, Executive Director of Publishing Technolog SUSAN CRESPI, Editorial Operations Manager; ALEX MORALES, Publishing Operations Manager; STAN LEE, Chairman Emeritus. For information regarding advertising in Marvel Comics or on Marvel.com, please contact Ni Disla, Director of Marvel Partnerships, at ndisla@marvel.com. For Marvel subscription inquiries, please call 800-217-9158. **Manufactured between 8/2/2013 and 9/16/2013 by R.R. DONNELLEY, INC., SALEM, VA, US**

10 9 8 7 6 5 4 3 2 1

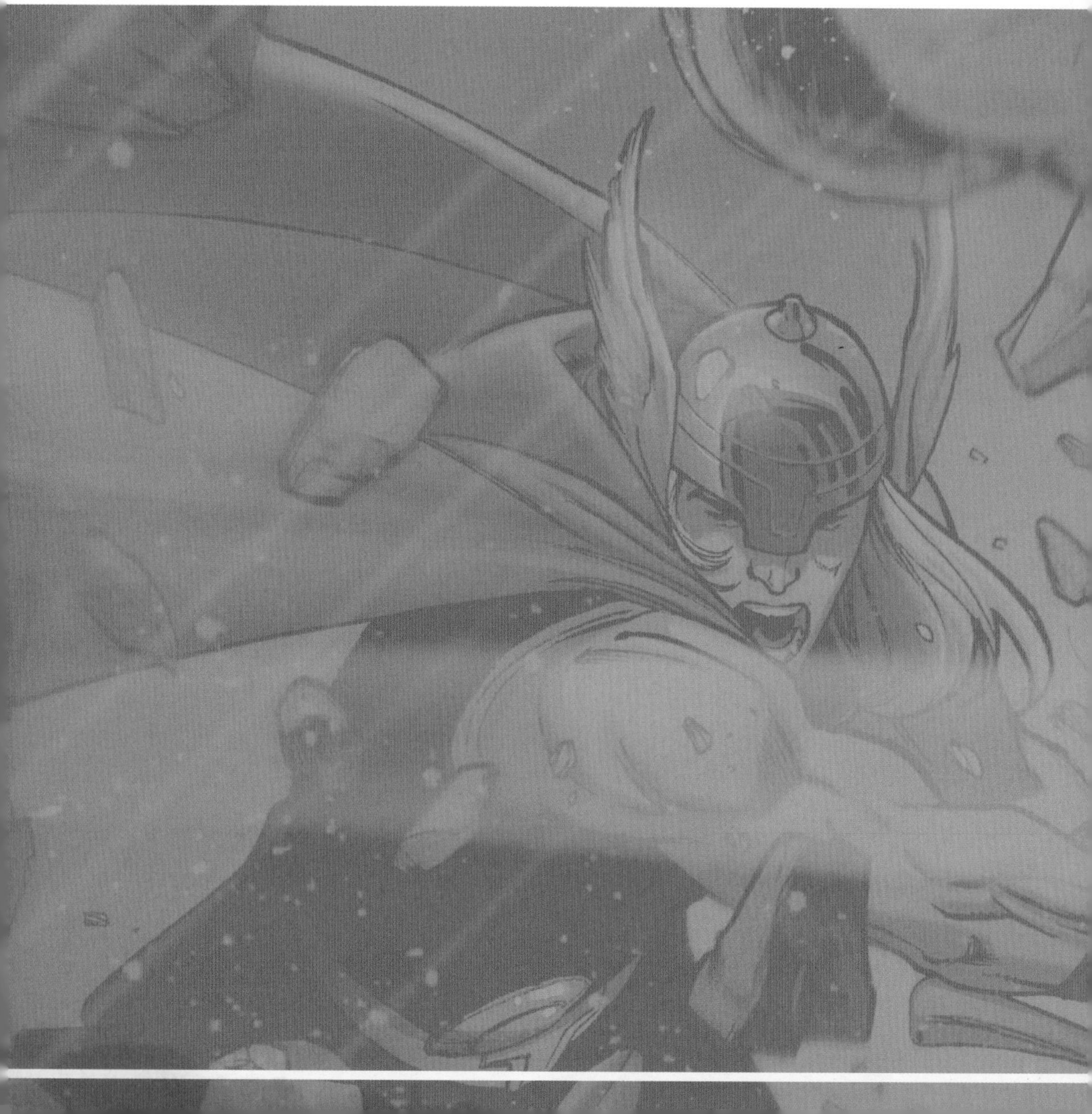

THOR

WRITER
MATTHEW STURGES

ARTIST
PEPE LARRAZ

COLOR ARTIST
WIL QUINTANA

LETTERER
VC'S CORY PETIT

COVER ARTIST
JULIAN TOTINO TEDESCO

ASSISTANT EDITORS
JAKE THOMAS WITH JON MOISAN

EDITOR
LAUREN SANKOVITCH

SEASON ONE

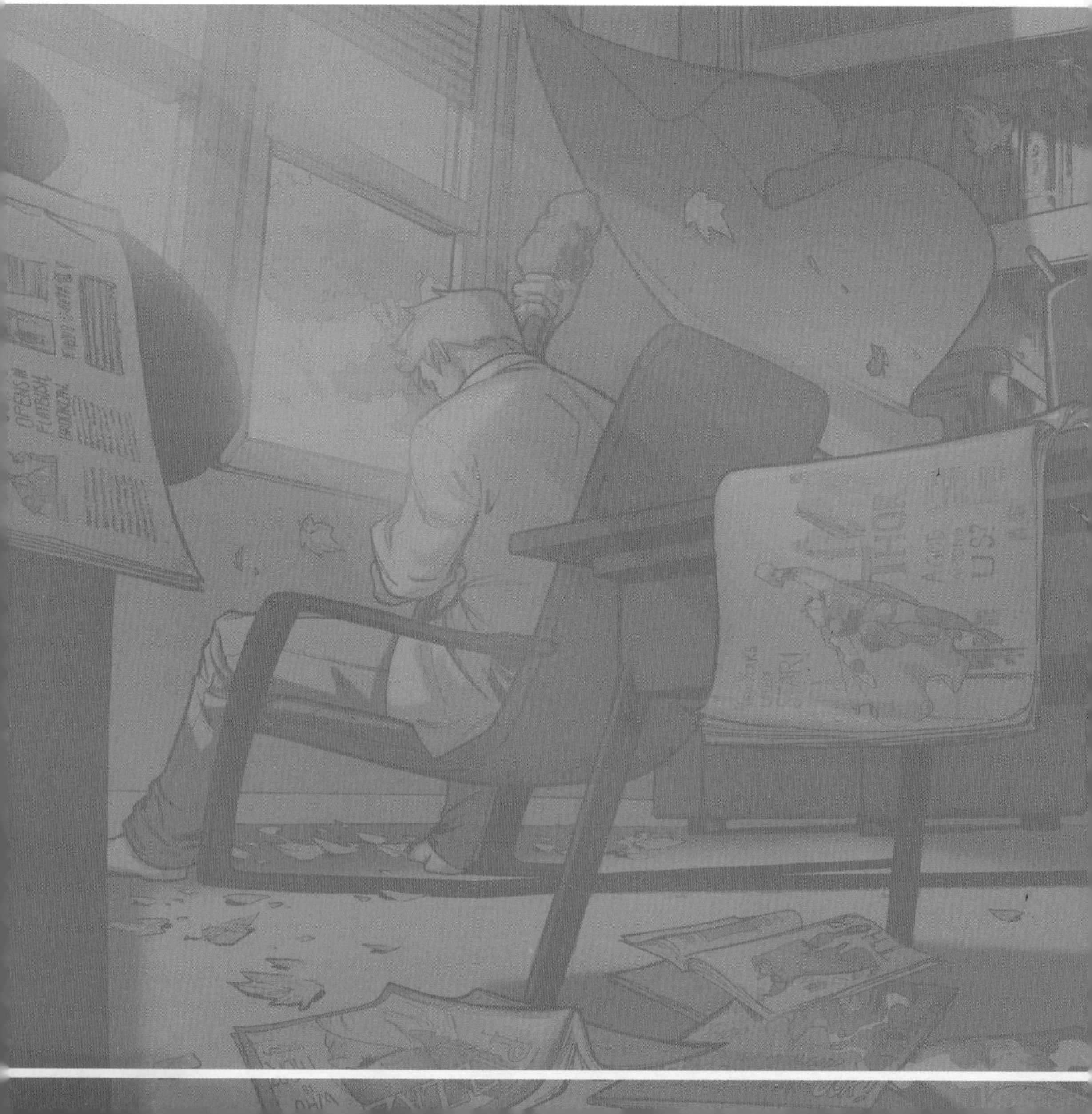

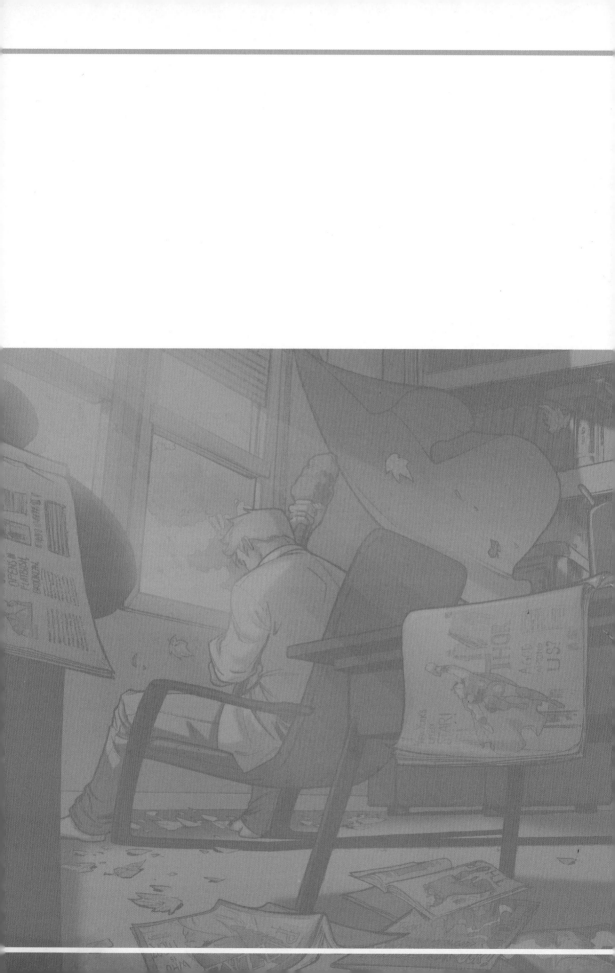

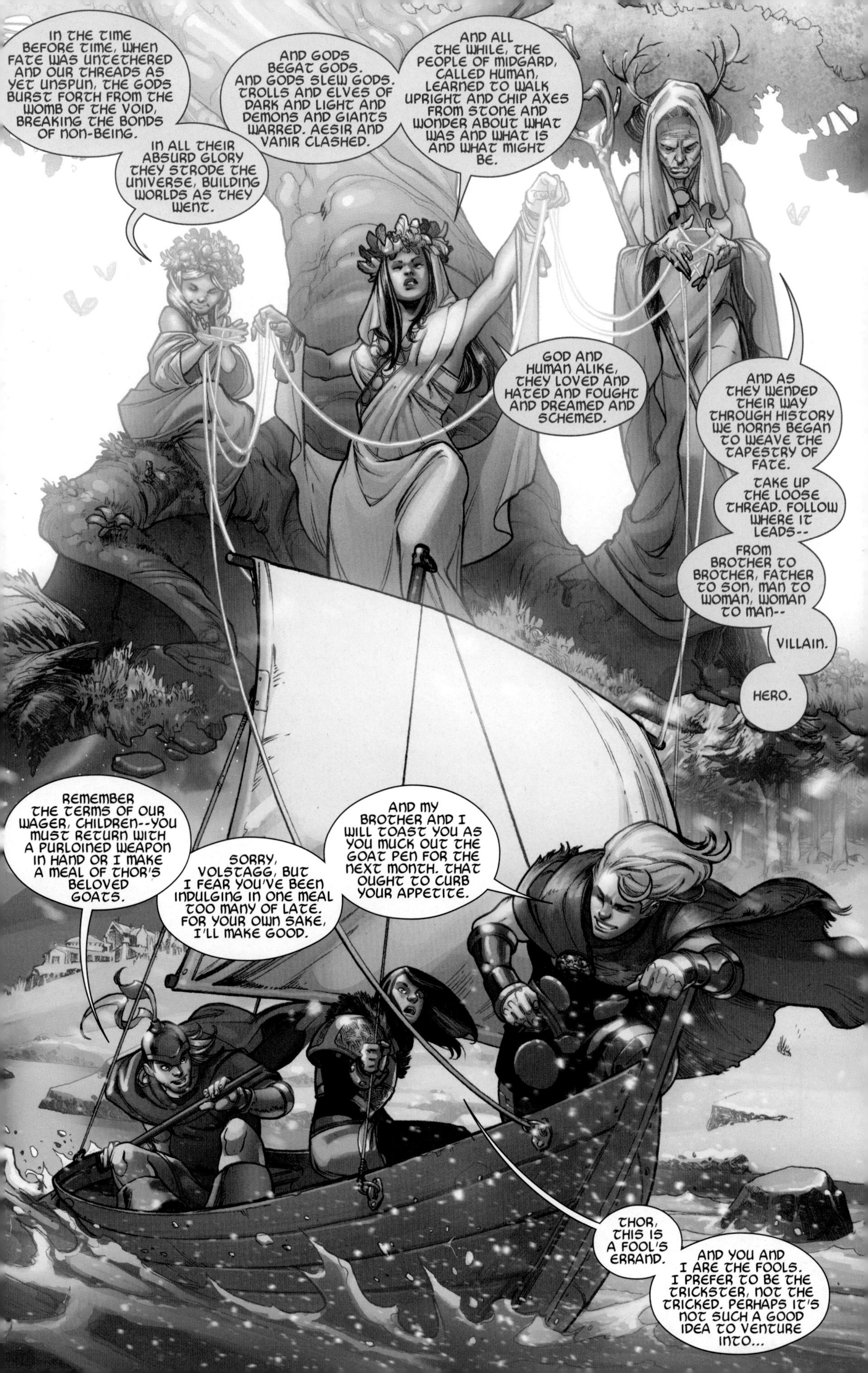
IN THE TIME BEFORE TIME, WHEN FATE WAS UNTETHERED AND OUR THREADS AS YET UNSPUN, THE GODS BURST FORTH FROM THE WOMB OF THE VOID, BREAKING THE BONDS OF NON-BEING.
IN ALL THEIR ABSURD GLORY THEY STRODE THE UNIVERSE, BUILDING WORLDS AS THEY WENT.
AND GODS BEGAT GODS. AND GODS SLEW GODS. TROLLS AND ELVES OF DARK AND LIGHT AND DEMONS AND GIANTS WARRED. AESIR AND VANIR CLASHED.
AND ALL THE WHILE, THE PEOPLE OF MIDGARD, CALLED HUMAN, LEARNED TO WALK UPRIGHT AND CHIP AXES FROM STONE AND WONDER ABOUT WHAT WAS AND WHAT IS AND WHAT MIGHT BE.
GOD AND HUMAN ALIKE, THEY LOVED AND HATED AND FOUGHT AND DREAMED AND SCHEMED.
AND AS THEY WENDED THEIR WAY THROUGH HISTORY WE NORNS BEGAN TO WEAVE THE TAPESTRY OF FATE.
TAKE UP THE LOOSE THREAD. FOLLOW WHERE IT LEADS--
FROM BROTHER TO BROTHER, FATHER TO SON, MAN TO WOMAN, WOMAN TO MAN--
VILLAIN.
HERO.
REMEMBER THE TERMS OF OUR WAGER, CHILDREN--YOU MUST RETURN WITH A PURLOINED WEAPON IN HAND OR I MAKE A MEAL OF THOR'S BELOVED GOATS.
SORRY, VOLSTAGG, BUT I FEAR YOU'VE BEEN INDULGING IN ONE MEAL TOO MANY OF LATE. FOR YOUR OWN SAKE, I'LL MAKE GOOD.
AND MY BROTHER AND I WILL TOAST YOU AS YOU MUCK OUT THE GOAT PEN FOR THE NEXT MONTH. THAT OUGHT TO CURB YOUR APPETITE.
THOR, THIS IS A FOOL'S ERRAND.
AND YOU AND I ARE THE FOOLS. I PREFER TO BE THE TRICKSTER, NOT THE TRICKED. PERHAPS IT'S NOT SUCH A GOOD IDEA TO VENTURE INTO...

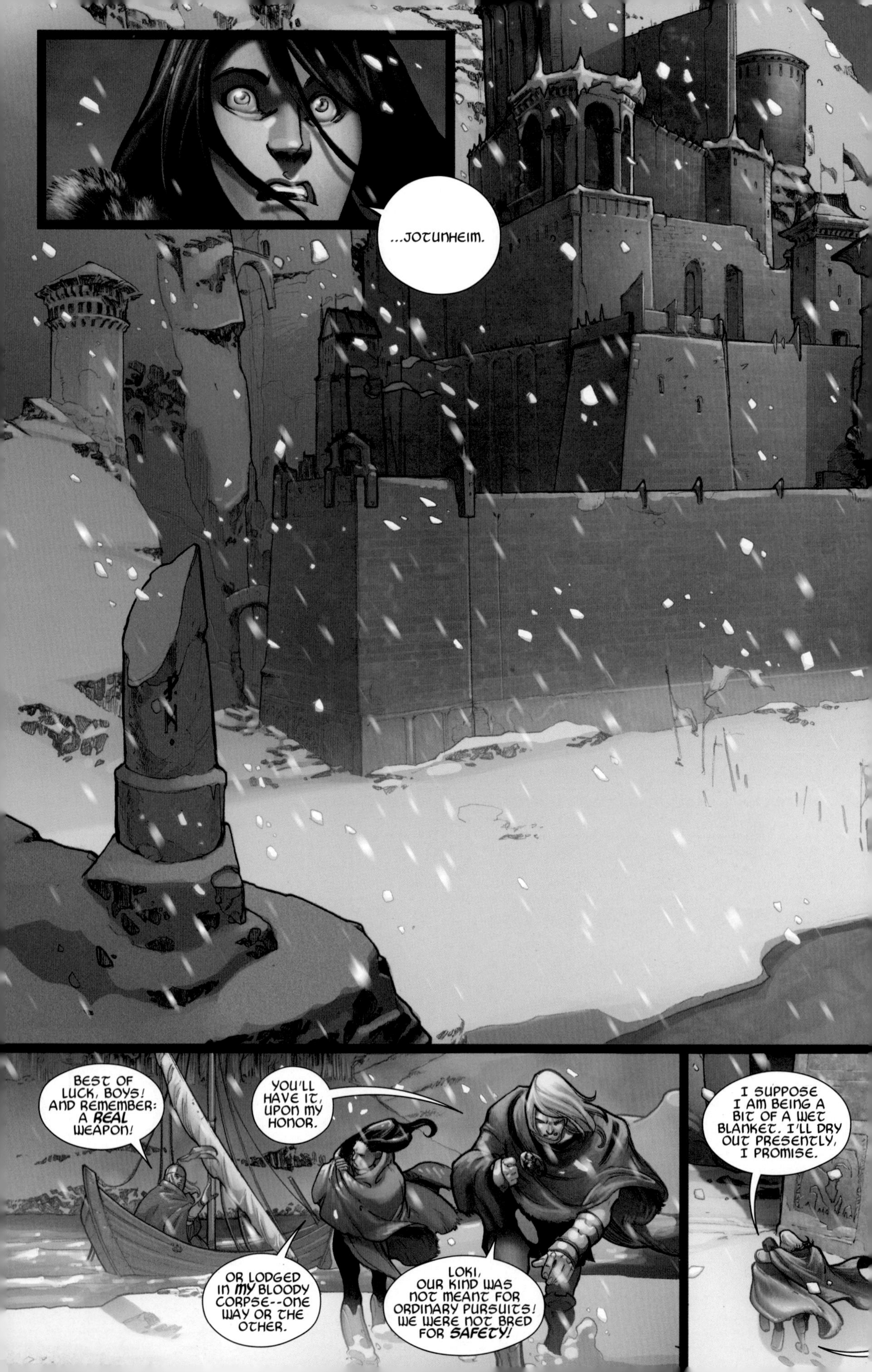
...JOTUNHEIM.
BEST OF LUCK, BOYS! AND REMEMBER: A REAL WEAPON!
YOU'LL HAVE IT, UPON MY HONOR.
OR LODGED IN MY BLOODY CORPSE--ONE WAY OR THE OTHER.
LOKI, OUR KIND WAS NOT MEANT FOR ORDINARY PURSUITS! WE WERE NOT BRED FOR SAFETY!
I SUPPOSE I AM BEING A BIT OF A WET BLANKET. I'LL DRY OUT PRESENTLY, I PROMISE.

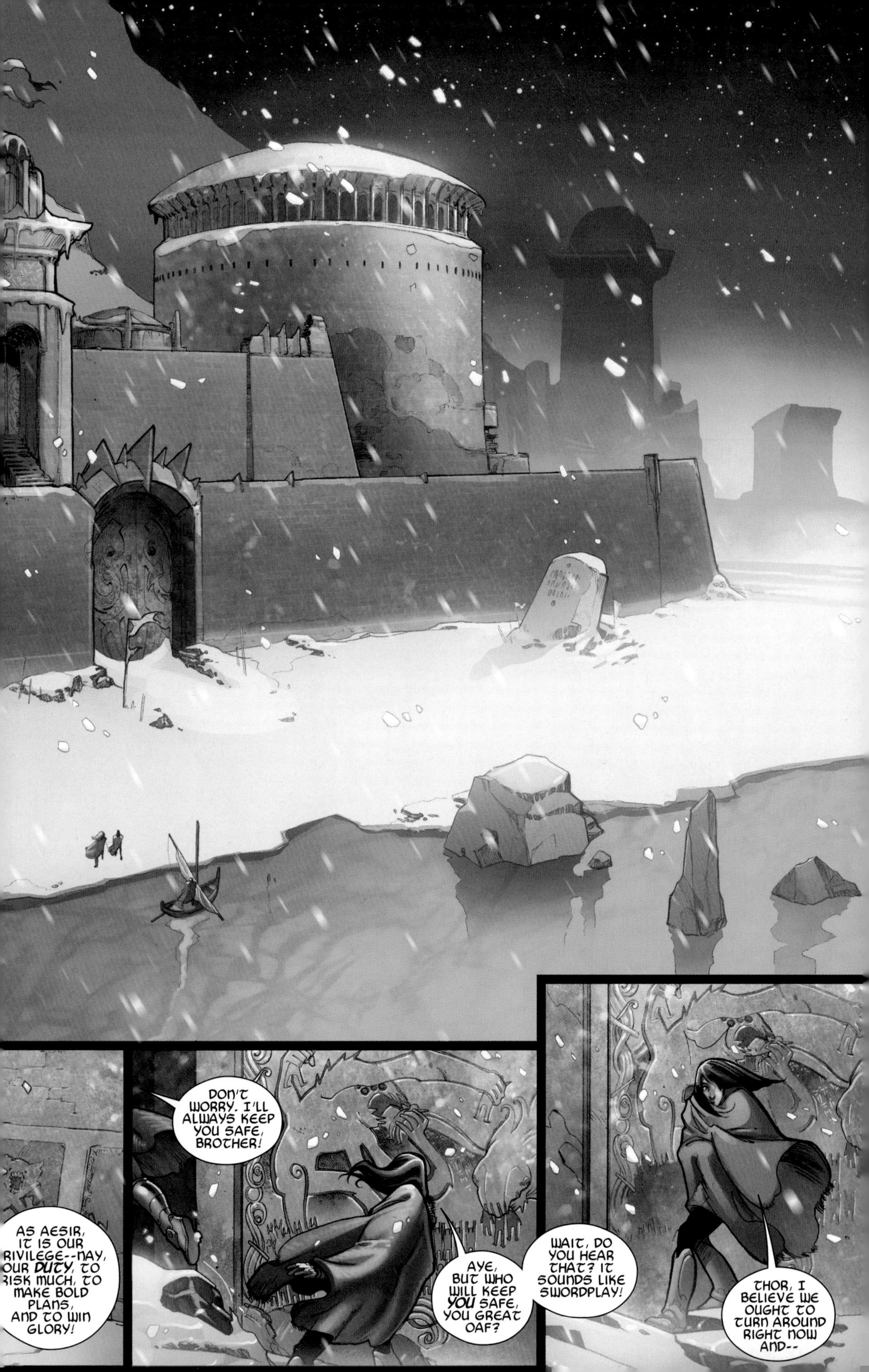

AS AESIR, IT IS OUR PRIVILEGE--NAY, OUR ***DUTY***, TO RISK MUCH, TO MAKE BOLD PLANS, AND TO WIN GLORY!
DON'T WORRY. I'LL ALWAYS KEEP YOU SAFE, BROTHER!
AYE, BUT WHO WILL KEEP ***YOU*** SAFE, YOU GREAT OAF?
WAIT, DO YOU HEAR THAT? IT SOUNDS LIKE SWORDPLAY!
THOR, I BELIEVE WE OUGHT TO TURN AROUND RIGHT NOW AND--

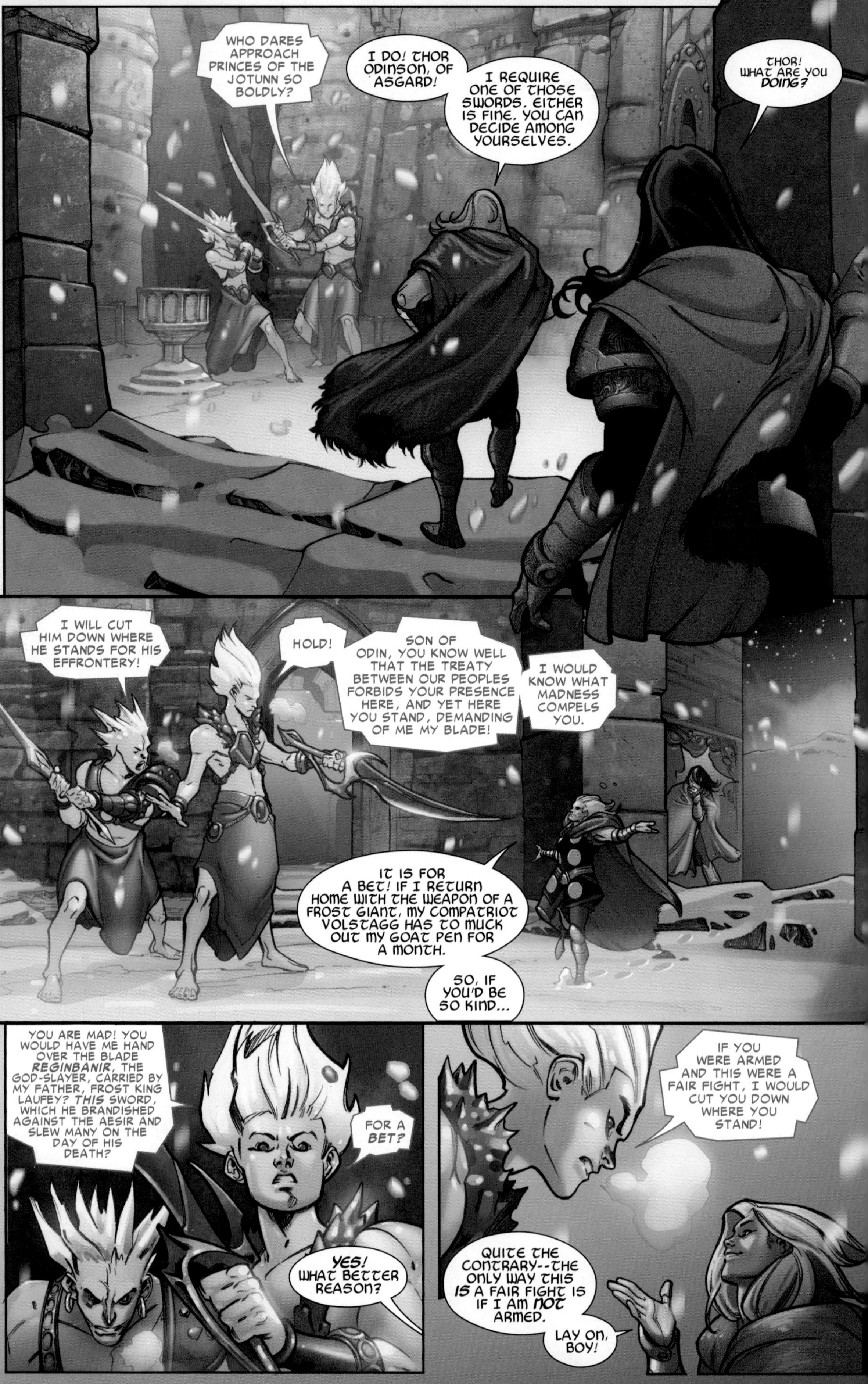

WHO DARES APPROACH PRINCES OF THE JOTUNN SO BOLDLY?
I DO! THOR ODINSON, OF ASGARD!
I REQUIRE ONE OF THOSE SWORDS. EITHER IS FINE. YOU CAN DECIDE AMONG YOURSELVES.
THOR! WHAT ARE YOU DOING?
I WILL CUT HIM DOWN WHERE HE STANDS FOR HIS EFFRONTERY!
HOLD!
SON OF ODIN, YOU KNOW WELL THAT THE TREATY BETWEEN OUR PEOPLES FORBIDS YOUR PRESENCE HERE, AND YET HERE YOU STAND, DEMANDING OF ME MY BLADE!
I WOULD KNOW WHAT MADNESS COMPELS YOU.
IT IS FOR A BET! IF I RETURN HOME WITH THE WEAPON OF A FROST GIANT, MY COMPATRIOT VOLSTAGG HAS TO MUCK OUT MY GOAT PEN FOR A MONTH.
SO, IF YOU'D BE SO KIND...
YOU ARE MAD! YOU WOULD HAVE ME HAND OVER THE BLADE REGINBANIR, THE GOD-SLAYER, CARRIED BY MY FATHER, FROST KING LAUFEY? THIS SWORD, WHICH HE BRANDISHED AGAINST THE AESIR AND SLEW MANY ON THE DAY OF HIS DEATH?
FOR A BET?
YES! WHAT BETTER REASON?
IF YOU WERE ARMED AND THIS WERE A FAIR FIGHT, I WOULD CUT YOU DOWN WHERE YOU STAND!
QUITE THE CONTRARY--THE ONLY WAY THIS IS A FAIR FIGHT IS IF I AM NOT ARMED.
LAY ON, BOY!

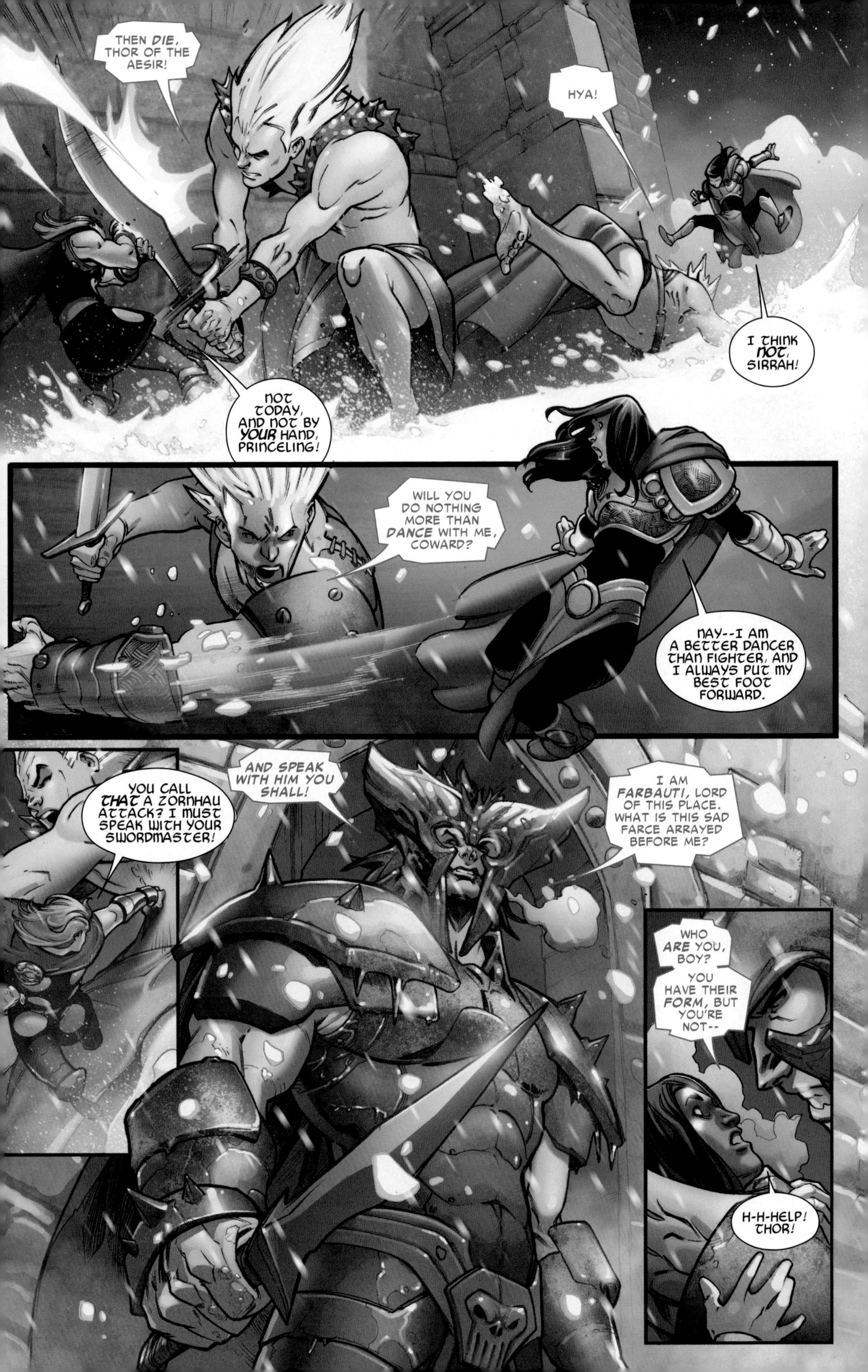
THEN DIE, THOR OF THE AESIR!
NOT TODAY, AND NOT BY YOUR HAND, PRINCELING!
HYA!
I THINK NOT, SIRRAH!
WILL YOU DO NOTHING MORE THAN DANCE WITH ME, COWARD?
NAY--I AM A BETTER DANCER THAN FIGHTER, AND I ALWAYS PUT MY BEST FOOT FORWARD.
YOU CALL THAT A ZORNHAU ATTACK? I MUST SPEAK WITH YOUR SWORDMASTER!
AND SPEAK WITH HIM YOU SHALL!
I AM FARBAUTI, LORD OF THIS PLACE. WHAT IS THIS SAD FARCE ARRAYED BEFORE ME?
WHO ARE YOU, BOY?
YOU HAVE THEIR FORM, BUT YOU'RE NOT--
H-H-HELP! THOR!

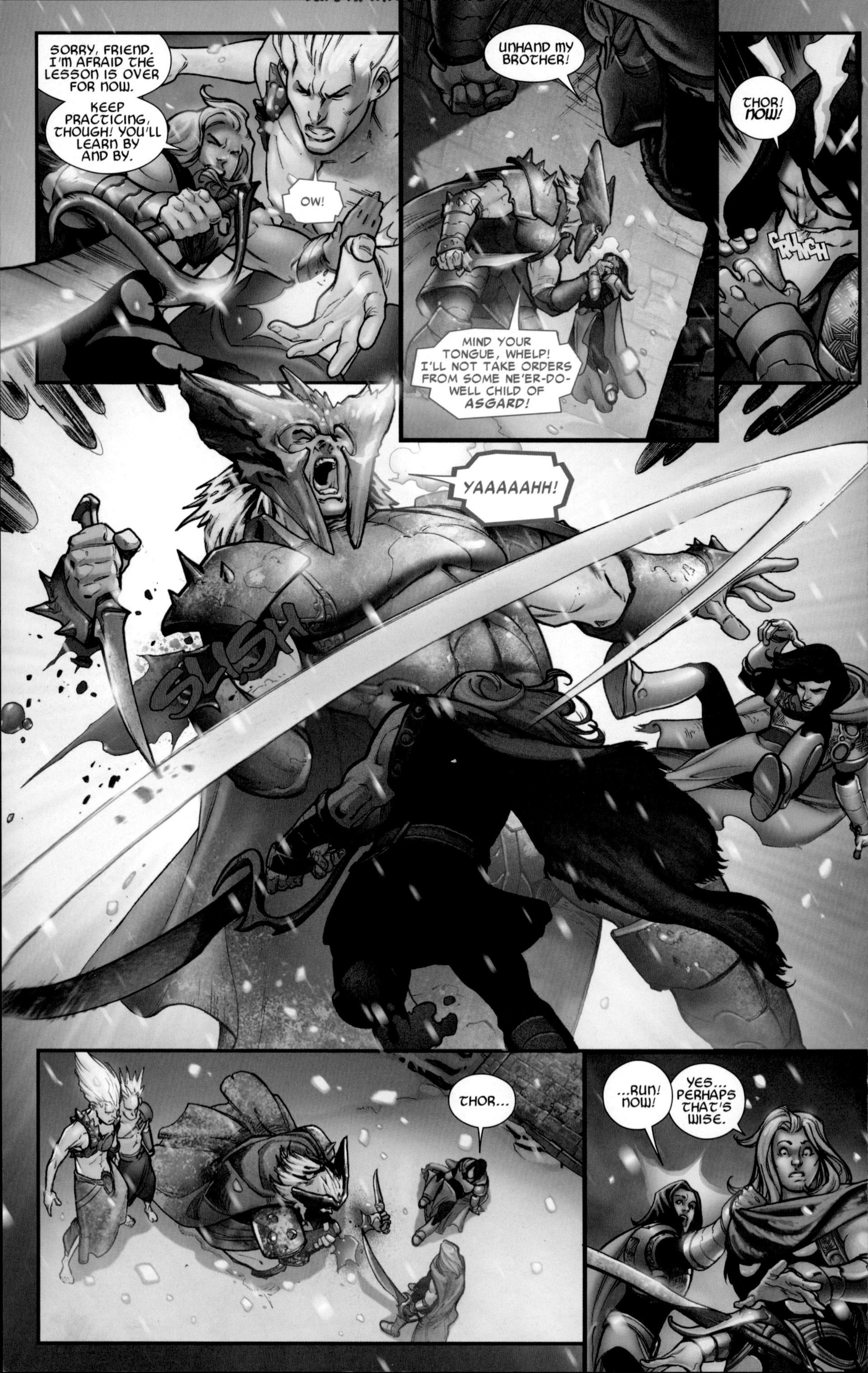
SORRY, FRIEND. I'M AFRAID THE LESSON IS OVER FOR NOW.
KEEP PRACTICING, THOUGH! YOU'LL LEARN BY AND BY.
OW!
UNHAND MY BROTHER!
MIND YOUR TONGUE, WHELP! I'LL NOT TAKE ORDERS FROM SOME NE'ER-DO-WELL CHILD OF ASGARD!
THOR! NOW!
CRUNCH
YAAAAAHH!
SLISH
THOR...
...RUN! NOW!
YES... PERHAPS THAT'S WISE.

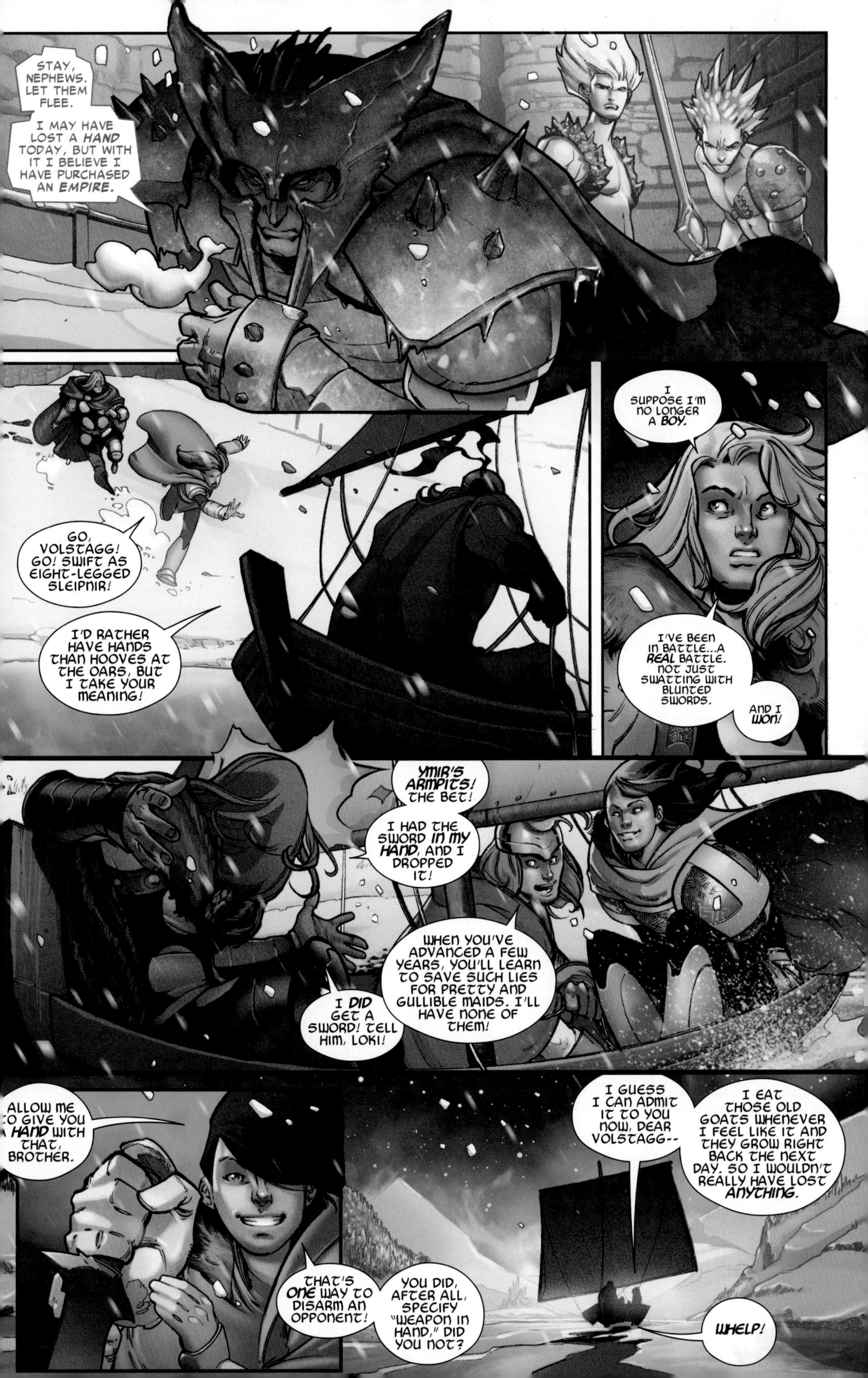
STAY, NEPHEWS. LET THEM FLEE.
I MAY HAVE LOST A HAND TODAY, BUT WITH IT I BELIEVE I HAVE PURCHASED AN EMPIRE.
GO, VOLSTAGG! GO! SWIFT AS EIGHT-LEGGED SLEIPNIR!
I'D RATHER HAVE HANDS THAN HOOVES AT THE OARS, BUT I TAKE YOUR MEANING!
I SUPPOSE I'M NO LONGER A BOY.
I'VE BEEN IN BATTLE...A REAL BATTLE. NOT JUST SWATTING WITH BLUNTED SWORDS.
AND I WON!
YMIR'S ARMPITS! THE BET!
I HAD THE SWORD IN MY HAND, AND I DROPPED IT!
WHEN YOU'VE ADVANCED A FEW YEARS, YOU'LL LEARN TO SAVE SUCH LIES FOR PRETTY AND GULLIBLE MAIDS. I'LL HAVE NONE OF THEM!
I DID GET A SWORD! TELL HIM, LOKI!
ALLOW ME TO GIVE YOU A HAND WITH THAT, BROTHER.
THAT'S ONE WAY TO DISARM AN OPPONENT!
YOU DID, AFTER ALL, SPECIFY "WEAPON IN HAND," DID YOU NOT?
I GUESS I CAN ADMIT IT TO YOU NOW, DEAR VOLSTAGG--
I EAT THOSE OLD GOATS WHENEVER I FEEL LIKE IT AND THEY GROW RIGHT BACK THE NEXT DAY. SO I WOULDN'T REALLY HAVE LOST ANYTHING.
WHELP!

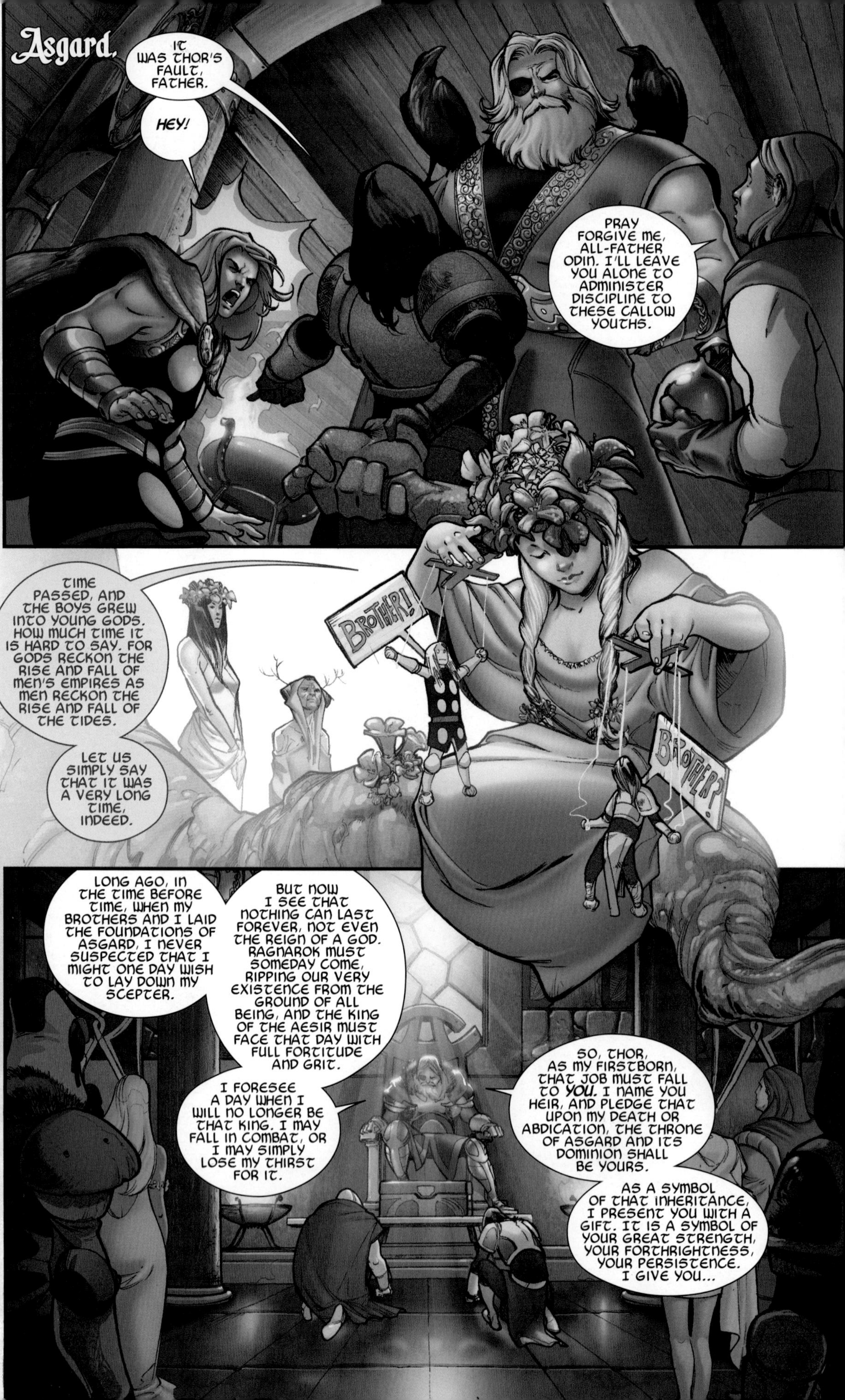

Asgard.
IT WAS THOR'S FAULT, FATHER.
HEY!
PRAY FORGIVE ME, ALL-FATHER ODIN. I'LL LEAVE YOU ALONE TO ADMINISTER DISCIPLINE TO THESE CALLOW YOUTHS.
TIME PASSED, AND THE BOYS GREW INTO YOUNG GODS. HOW MUCH TIME IT IS HARD TO SAY. FOR GODS RECKON THE RISE AND FALL OF MEN'S EMPIRES AS MEN RECKON THE RISE AND FALL OF THE TIDES.
LET US SIMPLY SAY THAT IT WAS A VERY LONG TIME, INDEED.
BROTHER!
BROTHER?
LONG AGO, IN THE TIME BEFORE TIME, WHEN MY BROTHERS AND I LAID THE FOUNDATIONS OF ASGARD, I NEVER SUSPECTED THAT I MIGHT ONE DAY WISH TO LAY DOWN MY SCEPTER.
BUT NOW I SEE THAT NOTHING CAN LAST FOREVER, NOT EVEN THE REIGN OF A GOD. RAGNAROK MUST SOMEDAY COME, RIPPING OUR VERY EXISTENCE FROM THE GROUND OF ALL BEING, AND THE KING OF THE AESIR MUST FACE THAT DAY WITH FULL FORTITUDE AND GRIT.
I FORESEE A DAY WHEN I WILL NO LONGER BE THAT KING. I MAY FALL IN COMBAT, OR I MAY SIMPLY LOSE MY THIRST FOR IT.
SO, THOR, AS MY FIRSTBORN, THAT JOB MUST FALL TO *YOU.* I NAME YOU HEIR, AND PLEDGE THAT UPON MY DEATH OR ABDICATION, THE THRONE OF ASGARD AND ITS DOMINION SHALL BE YOURS.
AS A SYMBOL OF THAT INHERITANCE, I PRESENT YOU WITH A GIFT. IT IS A SYMBOL OF YOUR GREAT STRENGTH, YOUR FORTHRIGHTNESS, YOUR PERSISTENCE. I GIVE YOU...

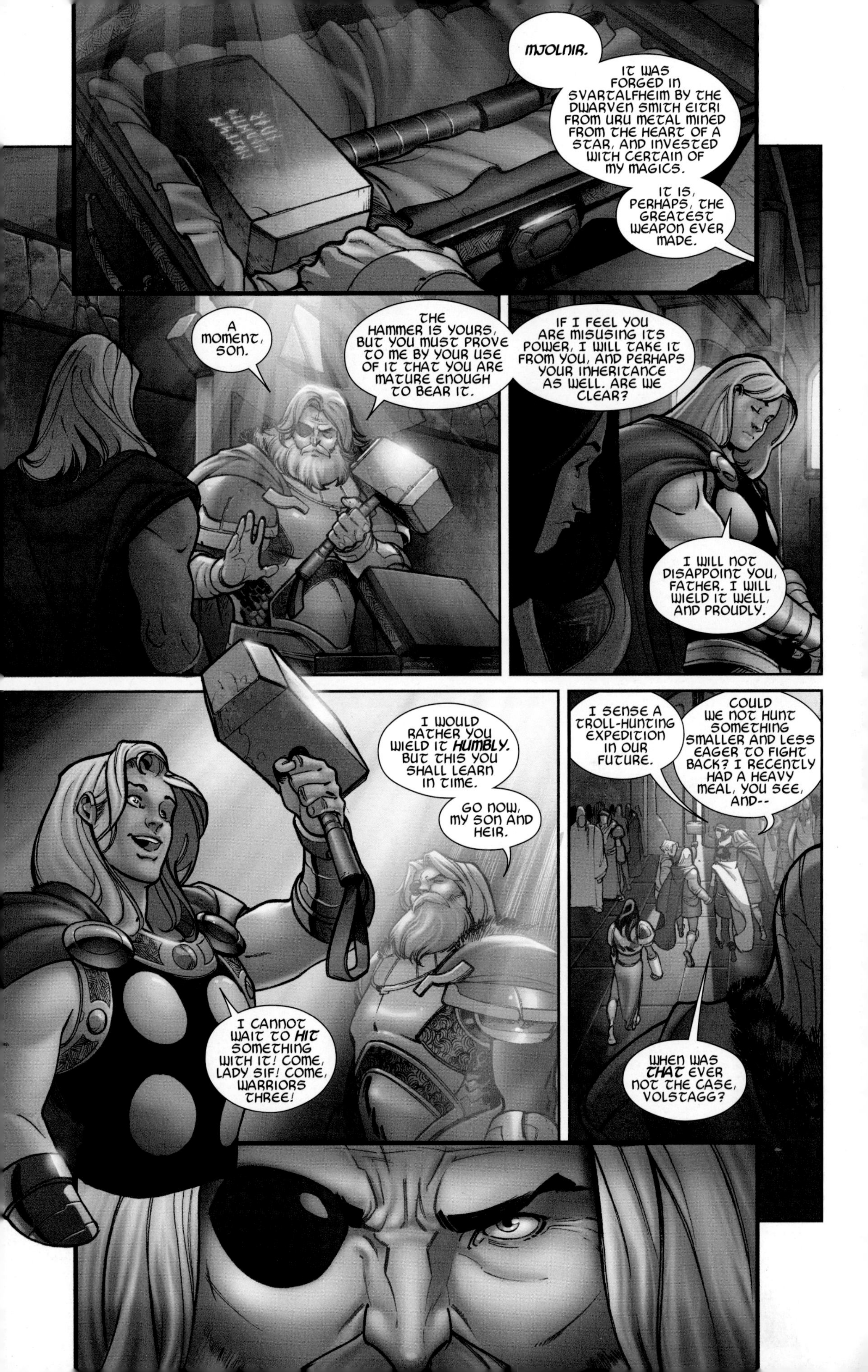
MJOLNIR.
IT WAS FORGED IN SVARTALFHEIM BY THE DWARVEN SMITH EITRI FROM URU METAL MINED FROM THE HEART OF A STAR, AND INVESTED WITH CERTAIN OF MY MAGICS.
IT IS, PERHAPS, THE GREATEST WEAPON EVER MADE.
A MOMENT, SON.
THE HAMMER IS YOURS, BUT YOU MUST PROVE TO ME BY YOUR USE OF IT THAT YOU ARE MATURE ENOUGH TO BEAR IT.
IF I FEEL YOU ARE MISUSING ITS POWER, I WILL TAKE IT FROM YOU, AND PERHAPS YOUR INHERITANCE AS WELL. ARE WE CLEAR?
I WILL NOT DISAPPOINT YOU, FATHER. I WILL WIELD IT WELL, AND PROUDLY.
I WOULD RATHER YOU WIELD IT HUMBLY. BUT THIS YOU SHALL LEARN IN TIME.
GO NOW, MY SON AND HEIR.
I CANNOT WAIT TO HIT SOMETHING WITH IT! COME, LADY SIF! COME, WARRIORS THREE!
I SENSE A TROLL-HUNTING EXPEDITION IN OUR FUTURE.
COULD WE NOT HUNT SOMETHING SMALLER AND LESS EAGER TO FIGHT BACK? I RECENTLY HAD A HEAVY MEAL, YOU SEE, AND--
WHEN WAS THAT EVER NOT THE CASE, VOLSTAGG?

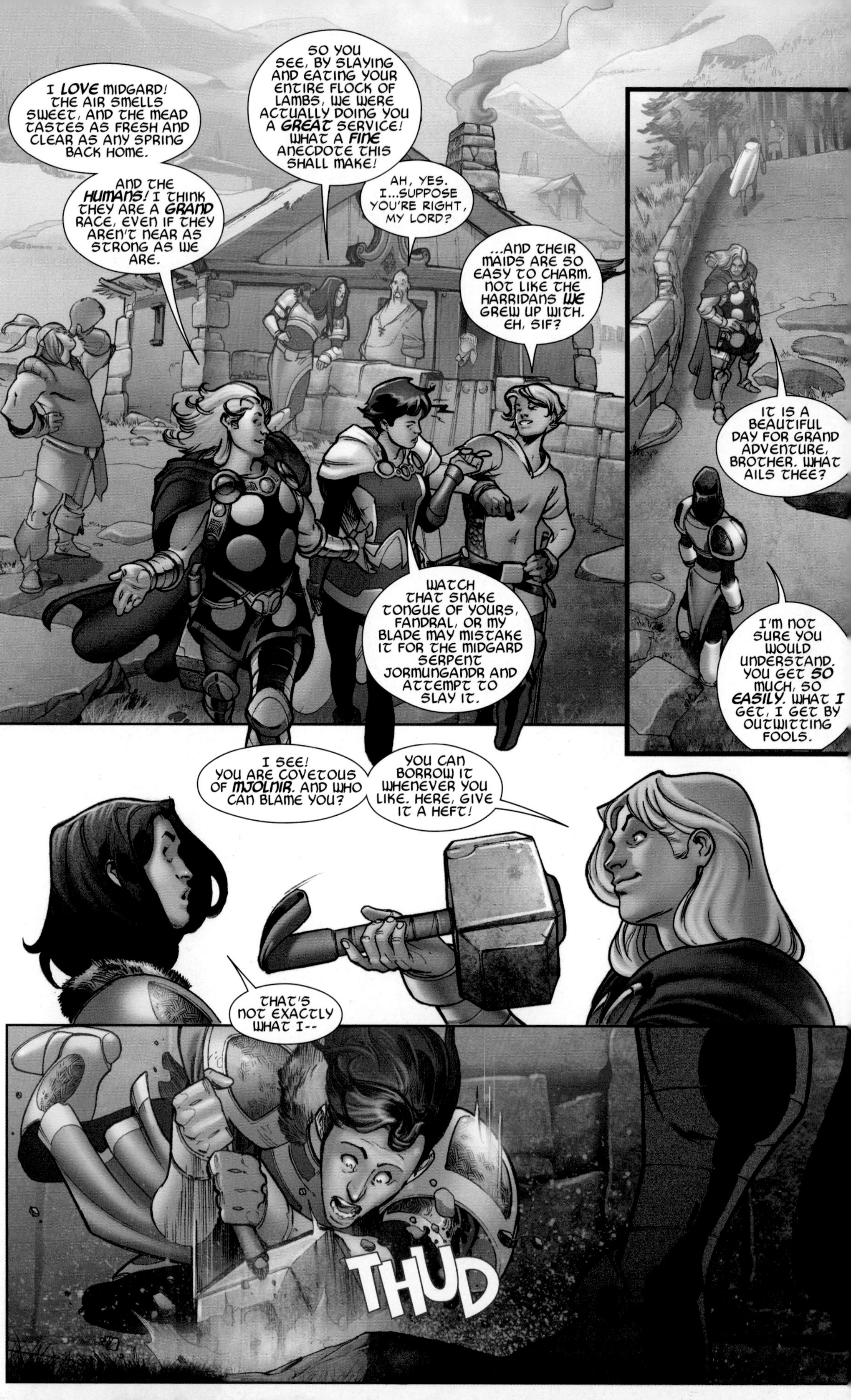
I LOVE MIDGARD! THE AIR SMELLS SWEET, AND THE MEAD TASTES AS FRESH AND CLEAR AS ANY SPRING BACK HOME.
AND THE HUMANS! I THINK THEY ARE A GRAND RACE, EVEN IF THEY AREN'T NEAR AS STRONG AS WE ARE.
SO YOU SEE, BY SLAYING AND EATING YOUR ENTIRE FLOCK OF LAMBS, WE WERE ACTUALLY DOING YOU A GREAT SERVICE! WHAT A FINE ANECDOTE THIS SHALL MAKE!
AH, YES. I...SUPPOSE YOU'RE RIGHT, MY LORD?
...AND THEIR MAIDS ARE SO EASY TO CHARM. NOT LIKE THE HARRIDANS WE GREW UP WITH. EH, SIF?
WATCH THAT SNAKE TONGUE OF YOURS, FANDRAL, OR MY BLADE MAY MISTAKE IT FOR THE MIDGARD SERPENT JORMUNGANDR AND ATTEMPT TO SLAY IT.
IT IS A BEAUTIFUL DAY FOR GRAND ADVENTURE, BROTHER. WHAT AILS THEE?
I'M NOT SURE YOU WOULD UNDERSTAND. YOU GET SO MUCH, SO EASILY. WHAT I GET, I GET BY OUTWITTING FOOLS.
I SEE! YOU ARE COVETOUS OF MJOLNIR. AND WHO CAN BLAME YOU?
YOU CAN BORROW IT WHENEVER YOU LIKE. HERE, GIVE IT A HEFT!
THAT'S NOT EXACTLY WHAT I--
THUD

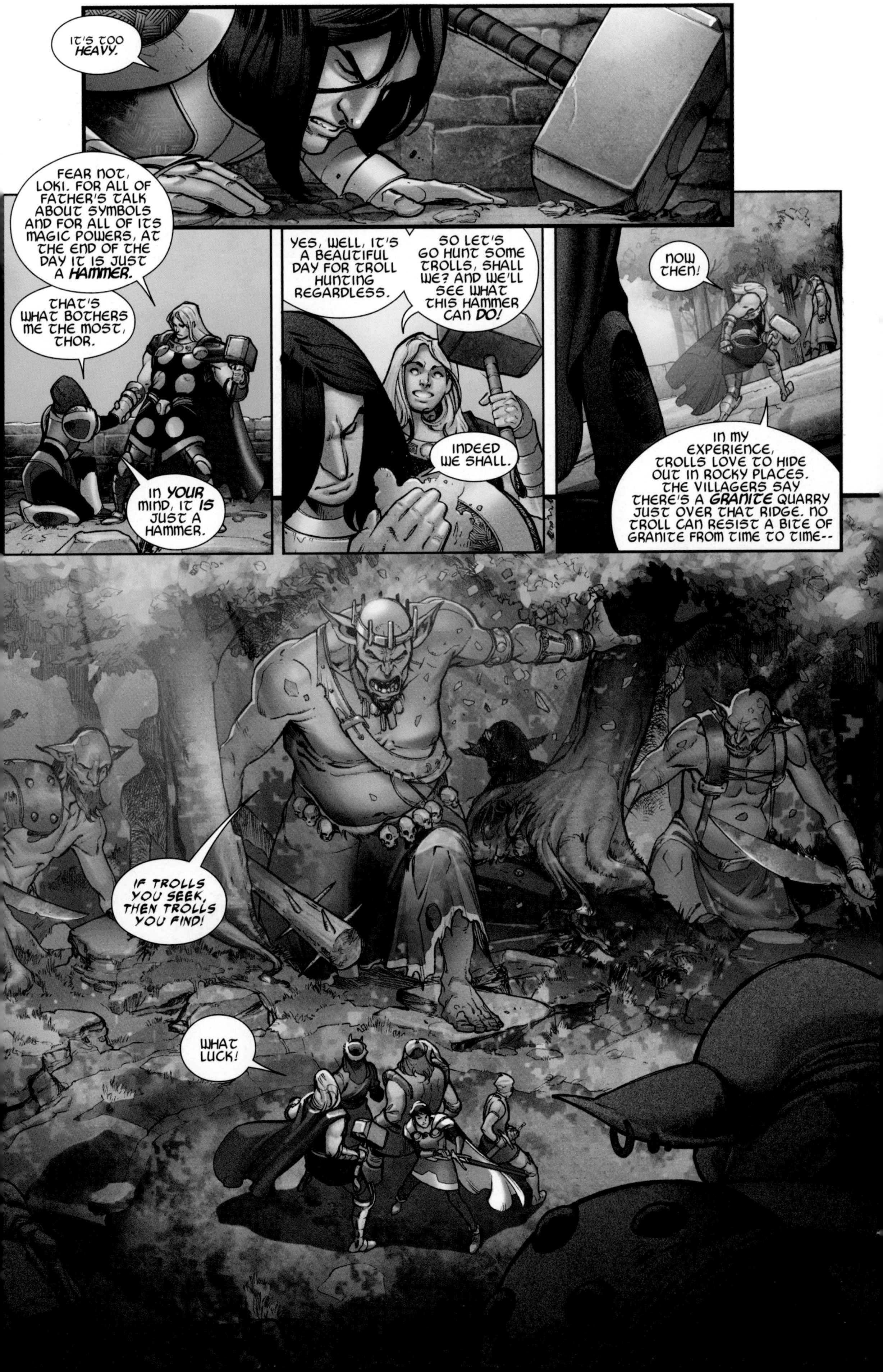
IT'S TOO HEAVY.
FEAR NOT, LOKI. FOR ALL OF FATHER'S TALK ABOUT SYMBOLS AND FOR ALL OF ITS MAGIC POWERS, AT THE END OF THE DAY IT IS JUST A HAMMER.
THAT'S WHAT BOTHERS ME THE MOST, THOR.
IN YOUR MIND, IT IS JUST A HAMMER.
YES, WELL, IT'S A BEAUTIFUL DAY FOR TROLL HUNTING REGARDLESS.
SO LET'S GO HUNT SOME TROLLS, SHALL WE? AND WE'LL SEE WHAT THIS HAMMER CAN DO!
INDEED WE SHALL.
NOW THEN!
IN MY EXPERIENCE, TROLLS LOVE TO HIDE OUT IN ROCKY PLACES. THE VILLAGERS SAY THERE'S A GRANITE QUARRY JUST OVER THAT RIDGE. NO TROLL CAN RESIST A BITE OF GRANITE FROM TIME TO TIME--
IF TROLLS YOU SEEK, THEN TROLLS YOU FIND!
WHAT LUCK!

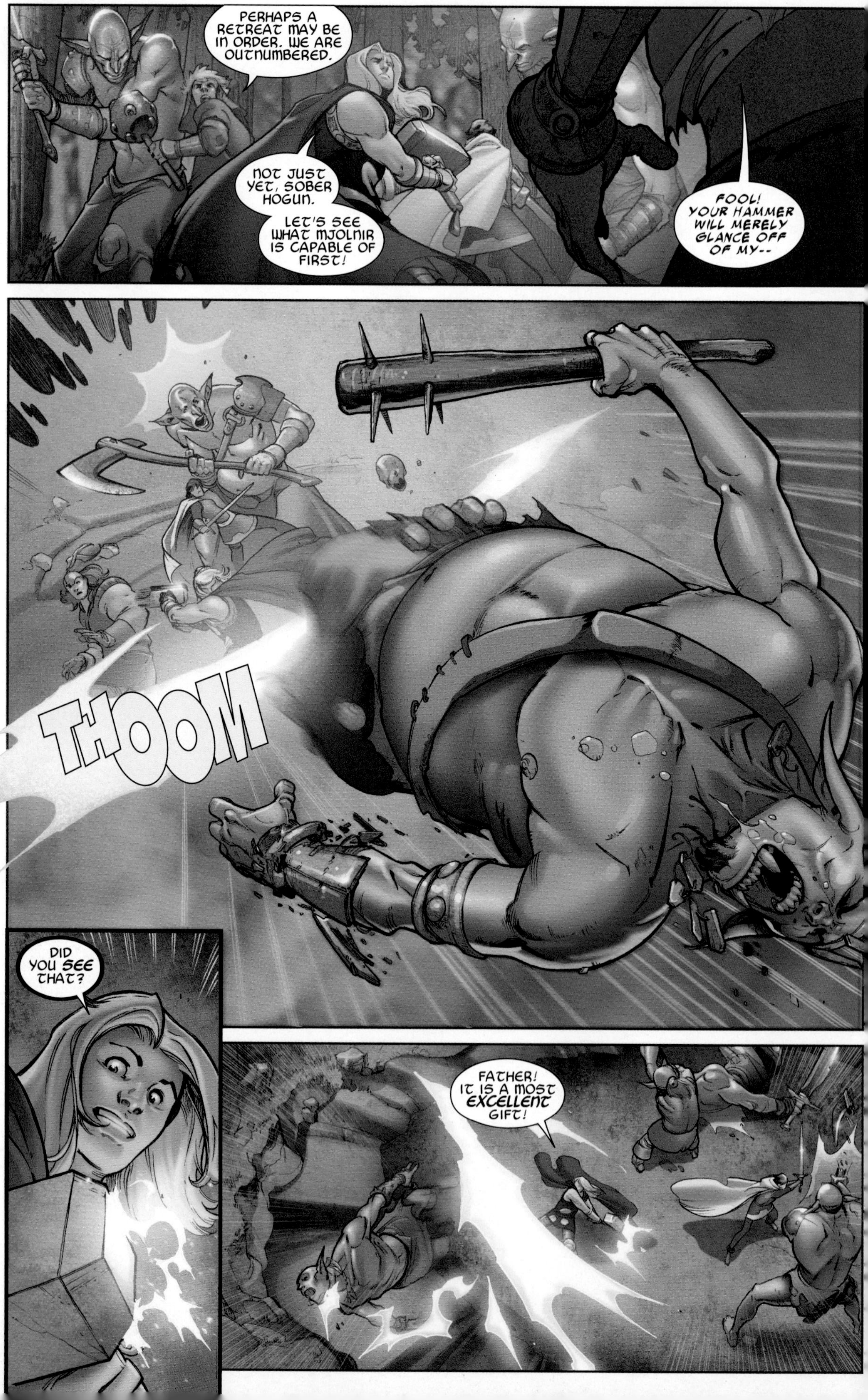
PERHAPS A RETREAT MAY BE IN ORDER. WE ARE OUTNUMBERED.
NOT JUST YET, SOBER HOGUN.
LET'S SEE WHAT MJOLNIR IS CAPABLE OF FIRST!
FOOL! YOUR HAMMER WILL MERELY GLANCE OFF OF MY--
THOOM
DID YOU SEE THAT?
FATHER! IT IS A MOST EXCELLENT GIFT!

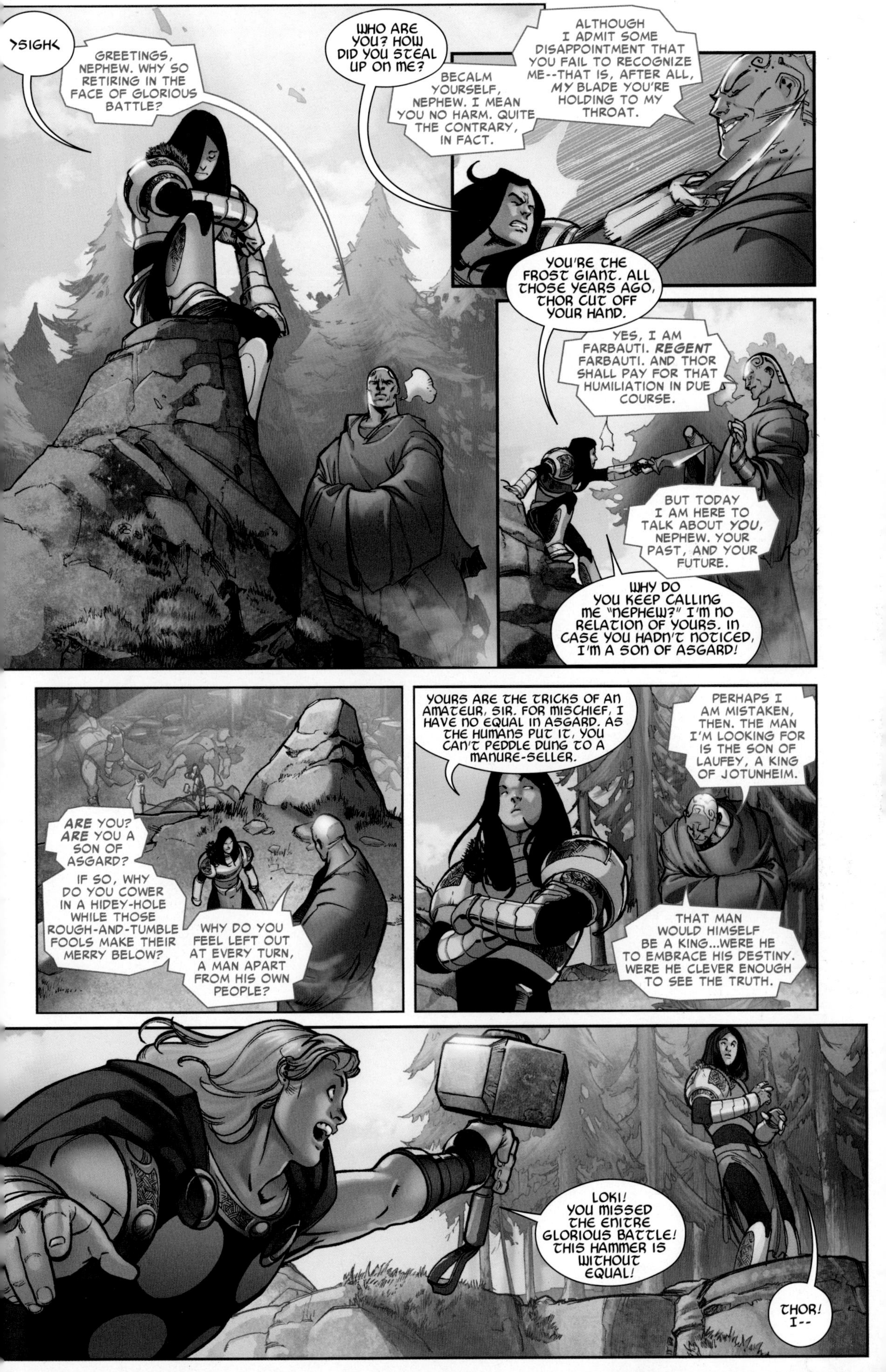
>SIGH<
GREETINGS, NEPHEW. WHY SO RETIRING IN THE FACE OF GLORIOUS BATTLE?
WHO ARE YOU? HOW DID YOU STEAL UP ON ME?
BECALM YOURSELF, NEPHEW. I MEAN YOU NO HARM. QUITE THE CONTRARY, IN FACT.
ALTHOUGH I ADMIT SOME DISAPPOINTMENT THAT YOU FAIL TO RECOGNIZE ME--THAT IS, AFTER ALL, *MY* BLADE YOU'RE HOLDING TO MY THROAT.
YOU'RE THE FROST GIANT. ALL THOSE YEARS AGO, THOR CUT OFF YOUR HAND.
YES, I AM FARBAUTI. ***REGENT*** FARBAUTI. AND THOR SHALL PAY FOR THAT HUMILIATION IN DUE COURSE.
BUT TODAY I AM HERE TO TALK ABOUT *YOU*, NEPHEW. YOUR PAST, AND YOUR FUTURE.
WHY DO YOU KEEP CALLING ME "NEPHEW?" I'M NO RELATION OF YOURS. IN CASE YOU HADN'T NOTICED, I'M A SON OF ASGARD!
ARE YOU? ***ARE*** YOU A SON OF ASGARD?
IF SO, WHY DO YOU COWER IN A HIDEY-HOLE WHILE THOSE ROUGH-AND-TUMBLE FOOLS MAKE THEIR MERRY BELOW?
WHY DO YOU FEEL LEFT OUT AT EVERY TURN, A MAN APART FROM HIS OWN PEOPLE?
YOURS ARE THE TRICKS OF AN AMATEUR, SIR. FOR MISCHIEF, I HAVE NO EQUAL IN ASGARD. AS THE HUMANS PUT IT, YOU CAN'T PEDDLE DUNG TO A MANURE-SELLER.
PERHAPS I AM MISTAKEN, THEN. THE MAN I'M LOOKING FOR IS THE SON OF LAUFEY, A KING OF JOTUNHEIM.
THAT MAN WOULD HIMSELF BE A KING...WERE HE TO EMBRACE HIS DESTINY. WERE HE CLEVER ENOUGH TO SEE THE TRUTH.
LOKI! YOU MISSED THE ENITRE GLORIOUS BATTLE! THIS HAMMER IS WITHOUT EQUAL!
THOR! I--

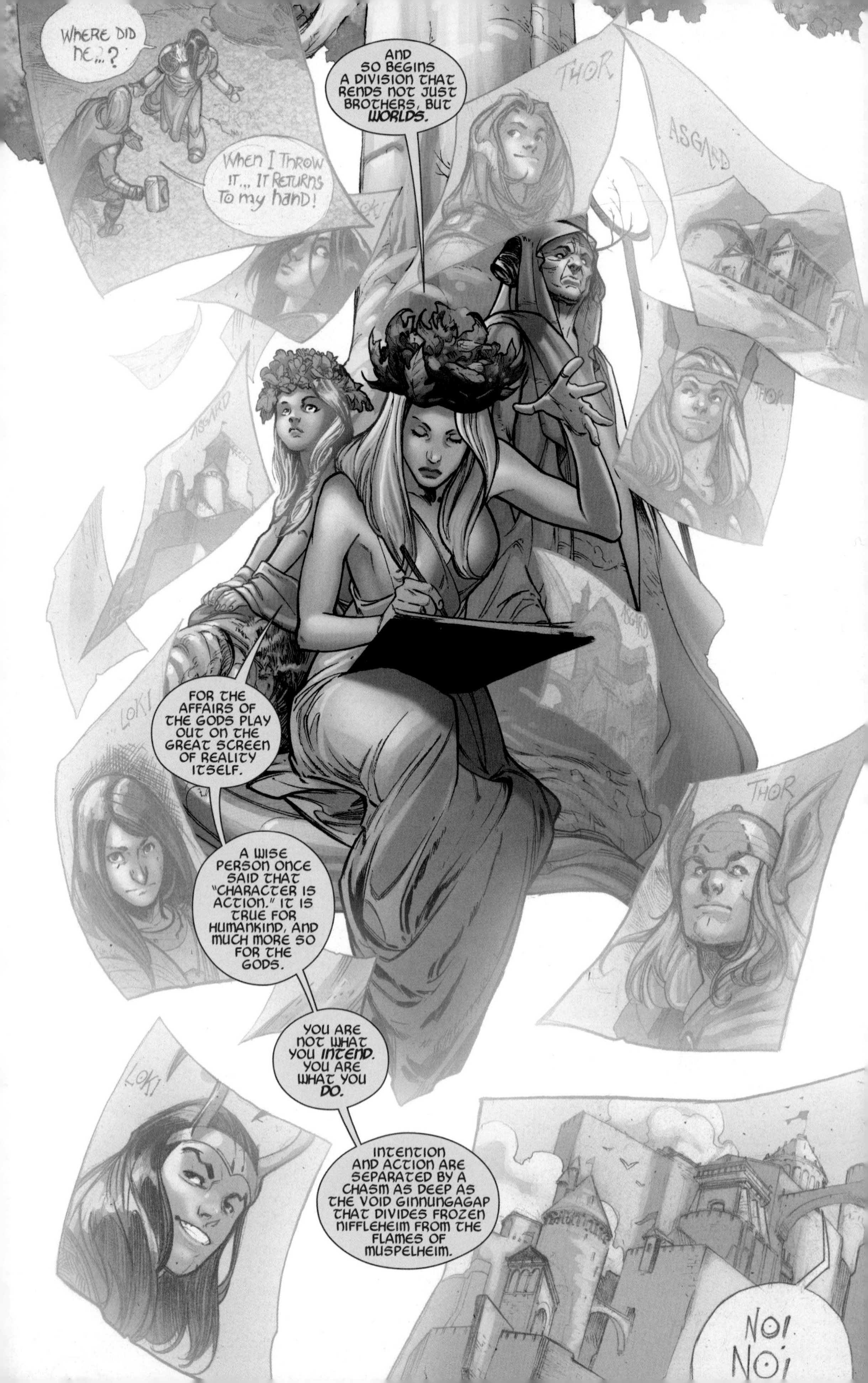
WHERE DID HE...?
WHEN I THROW IT... IT RETURNS TO MY HAND!
THOR
ASGARD
AND SO BEGINS A DIVISION THAT RENDS NOT JUST BROTHERS, BUT WORLDS.
THOR
ASGARD
ASGARD
LOKI
FOR THE AFFAIRS OF THE GODS PLAY OUT ON THE GREAT SCREEN OF REALITY ITSELF.
A WISE PERSON ONCE SAID THAT "CHARACTER IS ACTION." IT IS TRUE FOR HUMANKIND, AND MUCH MORE SO FOR THE GODS.
THOR
YOU ARE NOT WHAT YOU INTEND. YOU ARE WHAT YOU DO.
LOKI
INTENTION AND ACTION ARE SEPARATED BY A CHASM AS DEEP AS THE VOID GINNUNGAGAP THAT DIVIDES FROZEN NIFFLEHEIM FROM THE FLAMES OF MUSPELHEIM.
NO! NO!

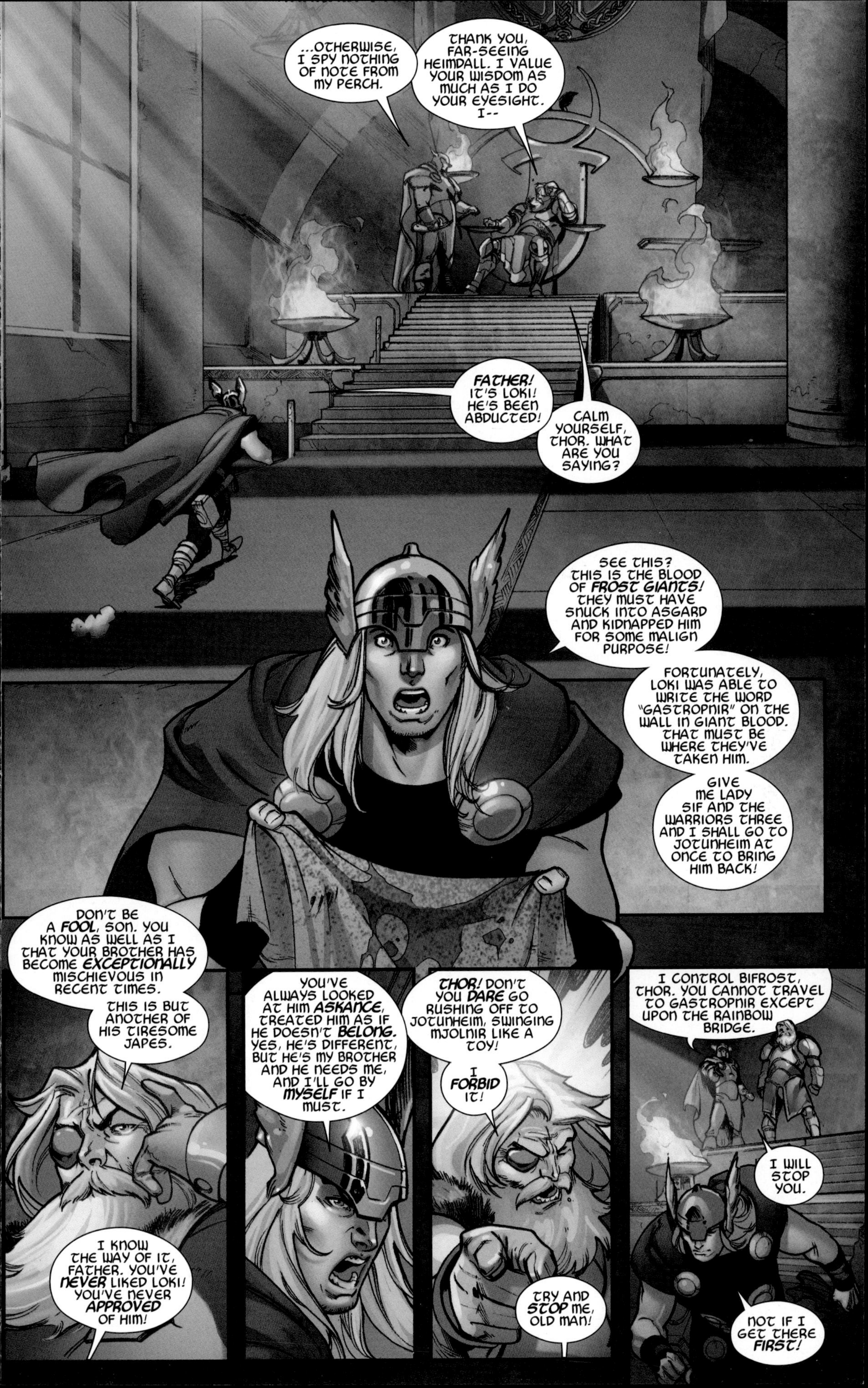
...OTHERWISE, I SPY NOTHING OF NOTE FROM MY PERCH.
THANK YOU, FAR-SEEING HEIMDALL. I VALUE YOUR WISDOM AS MUCH AS I DO YOUR EYESIGHT. I--
FATHER! IT'S LOKI! HE'S BEEN ABDUCTED!
CALM YOURSELF, THOR. WHAT ARE YOU SAYING?
SEE THIS? THIS IS THE BLOOD OF FROST GIANTS! THEY MUST HAVE SNUCK INTO ASGARD AND KIDNAPPED HIM FOR SOME MALIGN PURPOSE!
FORTUNATELY, LOKI WAS ABLE TO WRITE THE WORD "GASTROPNIR" ON THE WALL IN GIANT BLOOD. THAT MUST BE WHERE THEY'VE TAKEN HIM.
GIVE ME LADY SIF AND THE WARRIORS THREE AND I SHALL GO TO JOTUNHEIM AT ONCE TO BRING HIM BACK!
DON'T BE A FOOL, SON. YOU KNOW AS WELL AS I THAT YOUR BROTHER HAS BECOME EXCEPTIONALLY MISCHIEVOUS IN RECENT TIMES.
THIS IS BUT ANOTHER OF HIS TIRESOME JAPES.
I KNOW THE WAY OF IT, FATHER. YOU'VE NEVER LIKED LOKI! YOU'VE NEVER APPROVED OF HIM!
YOU'VE ALWAYS LOOKED AT HIM ASKANCE, TREATED HIM AS IF HE DOESN'T BELONG. YES, HE'S DIFFERENT, BUT HE'S MY BROTHER AND HE NEEDS ME, AND I'LL GO BY MYSELF IF I MUST.
THOR! DON'T YOU DARE GO RUSHING OFF TO JOTUNHEIM, SWINGING MJOLNIR LIKE A TOY!
I FORBID IT!
TRY AND STOP ME, OLD MAN!
I CONTROL BIFROST, THOR. YOU CANNOT TRAVEL TO GASTROPNIR EXCEPT UPON THE RAINBOW BRIDGE.
I WILL STOP YOU.
NOT IF I GET THERE FIRST!

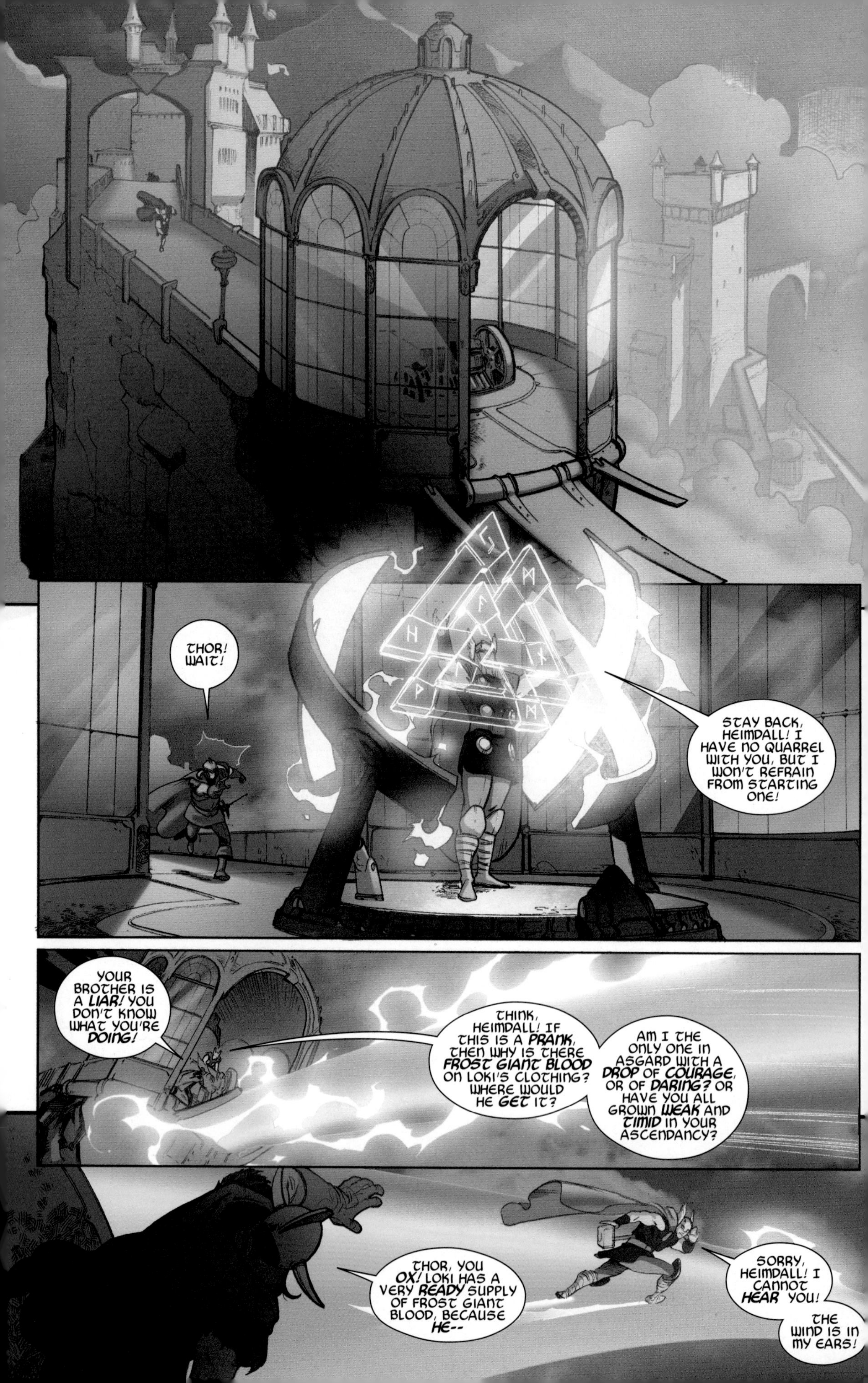
THOR! WAIT!
STAY BACK, HEIMDALL! I HAVE NO QUARREL WITH YOU, BUT I WON'T REFRAIN FROM STARTING ONE!
YOUR BROTHER IS A LIAR! YOU DON'T KNOW WHAT YOU'RE DOING!
THINK, HEIMDALL! IF THIS IS A PRANK, THEN WHY IS THERE FROST GIANT BLOOD ON LOKI'S CLOTHING? WHERE WOULD HE GET IT?
AM I THE ONLY ONE IN ASGARD WITH A DROP OF COURAGE, OR OF DARING? OR HAVE YOU ALL GROWN WEAK AND TIMID IN YOUR ASCENDANCY?
THOR, YOU OX! LOKI HAS A VERY READY SUPPLY OF FROST GIANT BLOOD, BECAUSE HE--
SORRY, HEIMDALL! I CANNOT HEAR YOU!
THE WIND IS IN MY EARS!

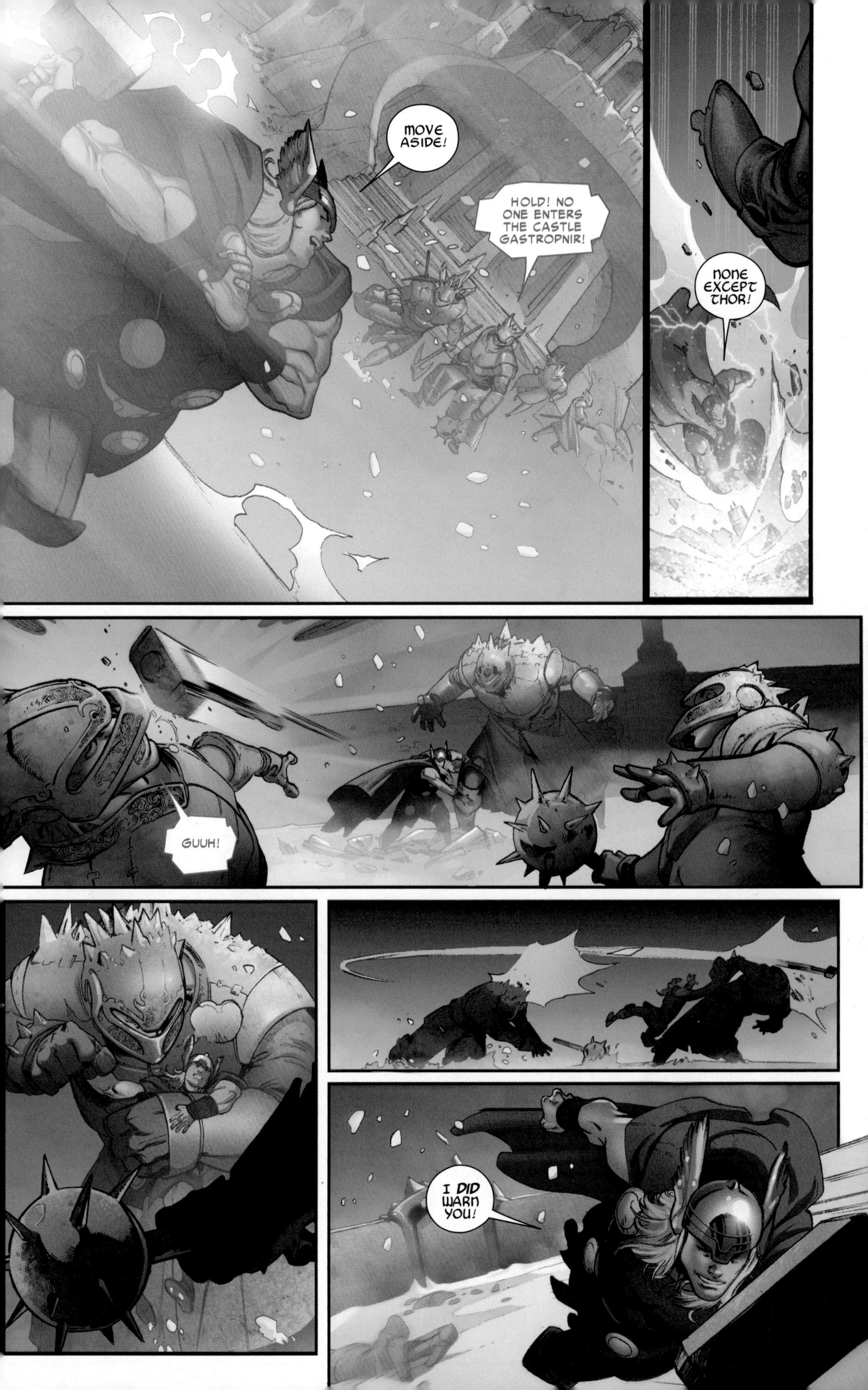
MOVE ASIDE!
HOLD! NO ONE ENTERS THE CASTLE GASTROPNIR!
NONE EXCEPT THOR!
GUUH!
I *DID* WARN YOU!

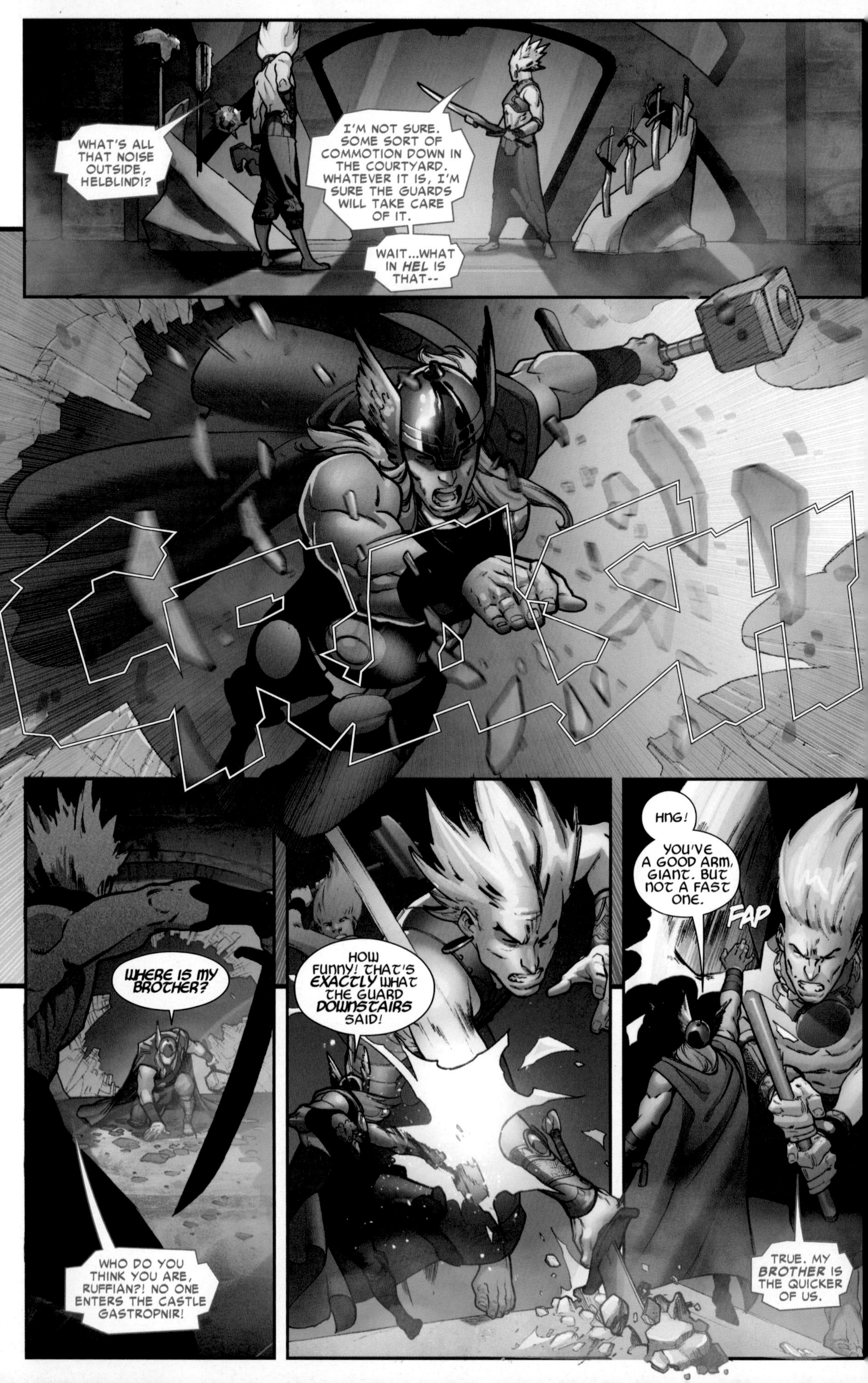
WHAT'S ALL THAT NOISE OUTSIDE, HELBLINDI?
I'M NOT SURE. SOME SORT OF COMMOTION DOWN IN THE COURTYARD. WHATEVER IT IS, I'M SURE THE GUARDS WILL TAKE CARE OF IT.
WAIT...WHAT IN HEL IS THAT--
CRAKSH!
WHERE IS MY BROTHER?
WHO DO YOU THINK YOU ARE, RUFFIAN?! NO ONE ENTERS THE CASTLE GASTROPNIR!
HOW FUNNY! THAT'S EXACTLY WHAT THE GUARD DOWNSTAIRS SAID!
HNG!
YOU'VE A GOOD ARM, GIANT. BUT NOT A FAST ONE.
FAP
TRUE. MY BROTHER IS THE QUICKER OF US.

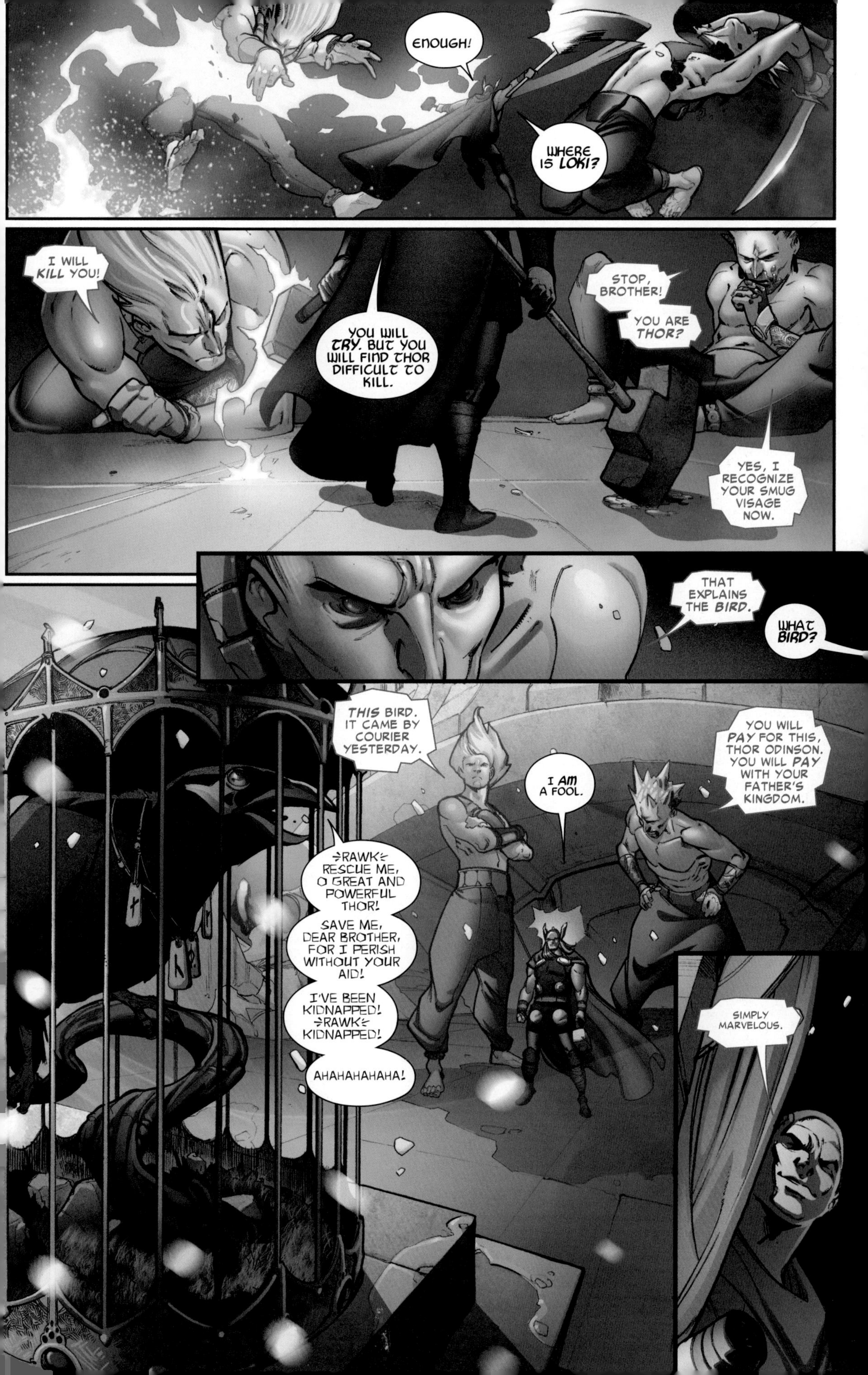
ENOUGH!
WHERE IS LOKI?
I WILL KILL YOU!
YOU WILL TRY. BUT YOU WILL FIND THOR DIFFICULT TO KILL.
STOP, BROTHER!
YOU ARE THOR?
YES, I RECOGNIZE YOUR SMUG VISAGE NOW.
THAT EXPLAINS THE BIRD.
WHAT BIRD?
THIS BIRD. IT CAME BY COURIER YESTERDAY.
I AM A FOOL.
YOU WILL PAY FOR THIS, THOR ODINSON. YOU WILL PAY WITH YOUR FATHER'S KINGDOM.
=RAWK= RESCUE ME, O GREAT AND POWERFUL THOR!
SAVE ME, DEAR BROTHER, FOR I PERISH WITHOUT YOUR AID!
I'VE BEEN KIDNAPPED! =RAWK= KIDNAPPED!
AHAHAHAHAHA!
SIMPLY MARVELOUS.

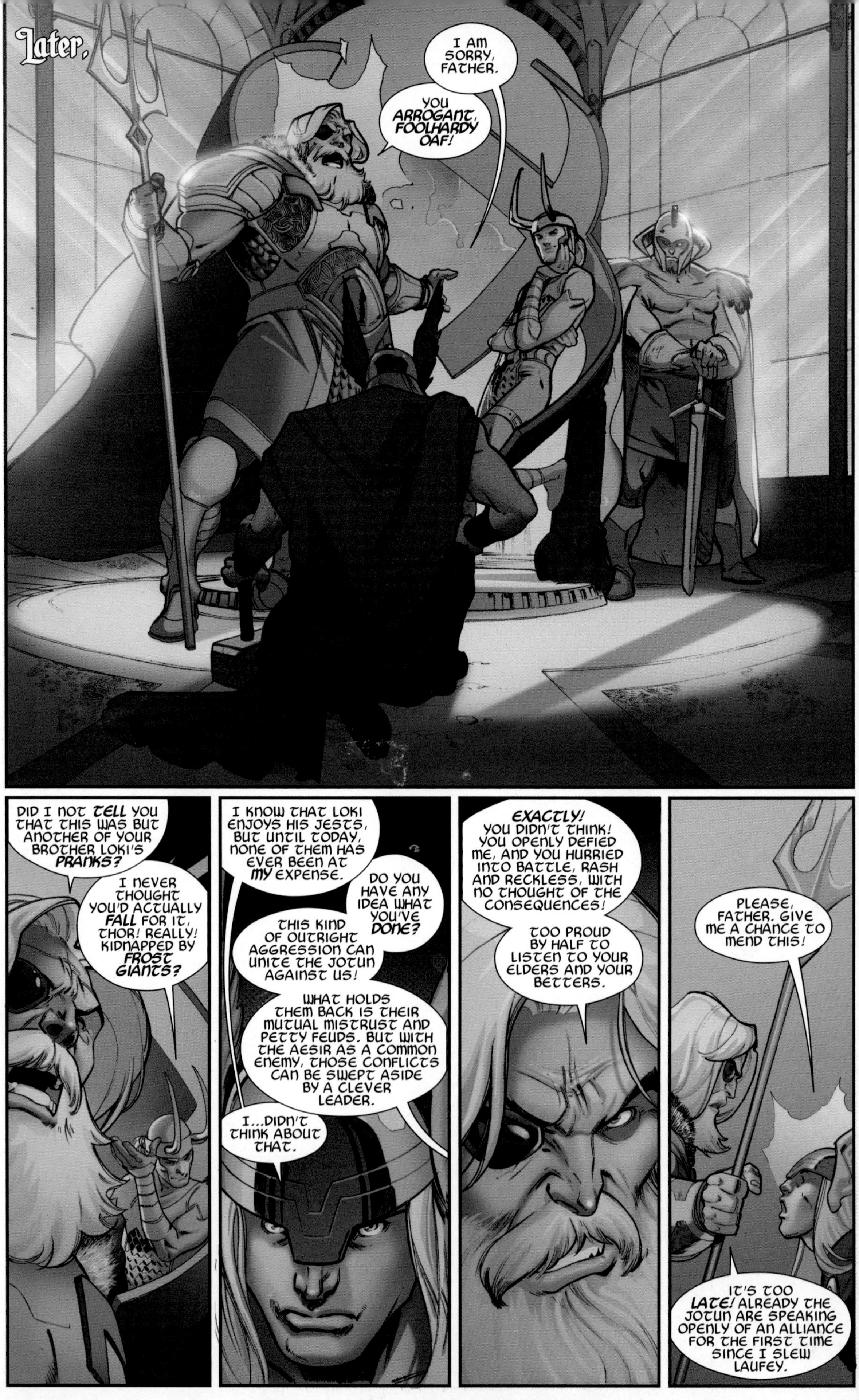
Later,
I AM SORRY, FATHER.
YOU ARROGANT, FOOLHARDY OAF!
DID I NOT TELL YOU THAT THIS WAS BUT ANOTHER OF YOUR BROTHER LOKI'S PRANKS?
I NEVER THOUGHT YOU'D ACTUALLY FALL FOR IT, THOR! REALLY! KIDNAPPED BY FROST GIANTS?
I KNOW THAT LOKI ENJOYS HIS JESTS, BUT UNTIL TODAY, NONE OF THEM HAS EVER BEEN AT MY EXPENSE.
DO YOU HAVE ANY IDEA WHAT YOU'VE DONE?
THIS KIND OF OUTRIGHT AGGRESSION CAN UNITE THE JOTUN AGAINST US!
WHAT HOLDS THEM BACK IS THEIR MUTUAL MISTRUST AND PETTY FEUDS. BUT WITH THE AESIR AS A COMMON ENEMY, THOSE CONFLICTS CAN BE SWEPT ASIDE BY A CLEVER LEADER.
I...DIDN'T THINK ABOUT THAT.
EXACTLY! YOU DIDN'T THINK! YOU OPENLY DEFIED ME, AND YOU HURRIED INTO BATTLE, RASH AND RECKLESS, WITH NO THOUGHT OF THE CONSEQUENCES!
TOO PROUD BY HALF TO LISTEN TO YOUR ELDERS AND YOUR BETTERS.
PLEASE, FATHER. GIVE ME A CHANCE TO MEND THIS!
IT'S TOO LATE! ALREADY THE JOTUN ARE SPEAKING OPENLY OF AN ALLIANCE FOR THE FIRST TIME SINCE I SLEW LAUFEY.

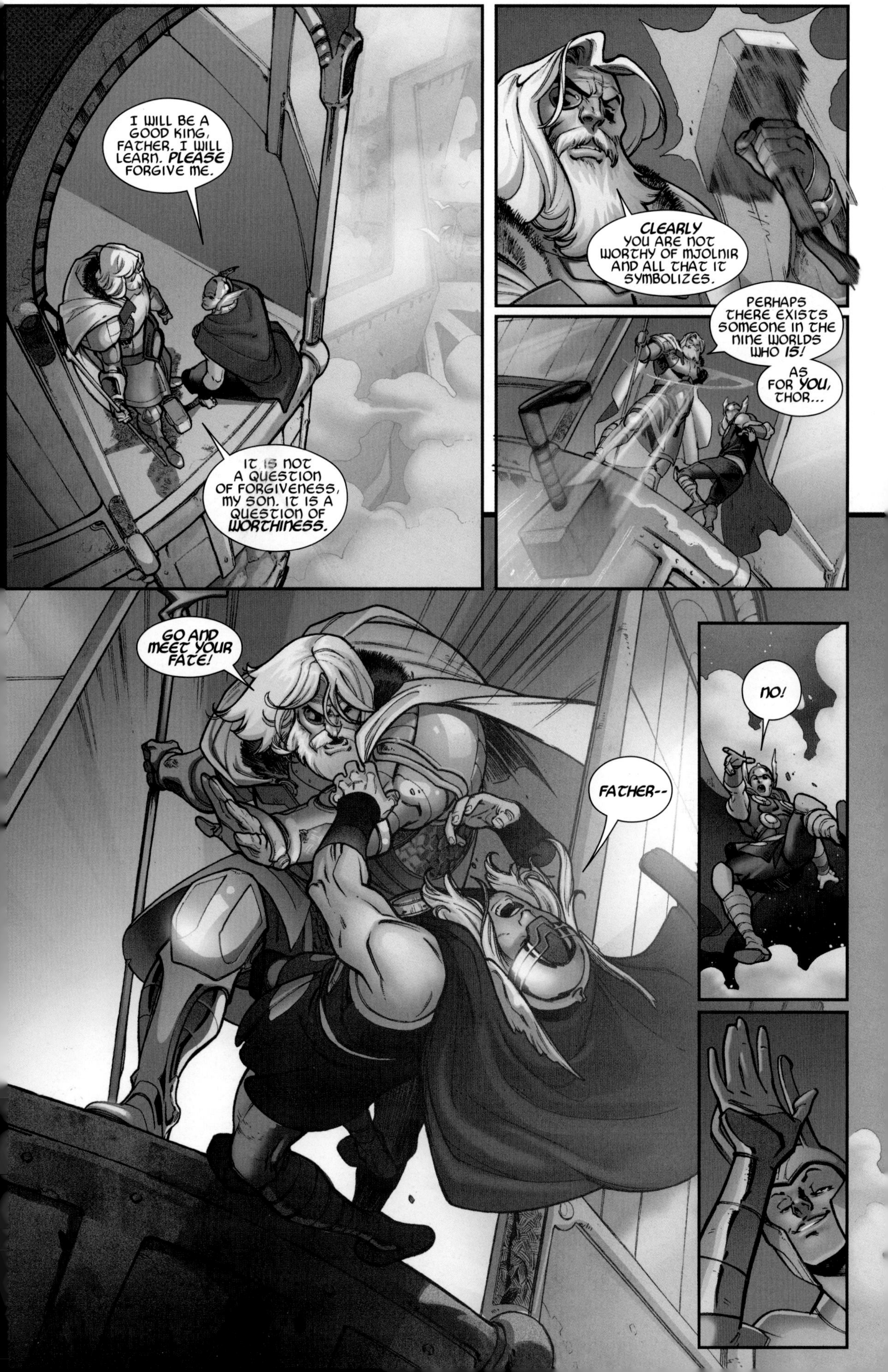
I WILL BE A GOOD KING, FATHER. I WILL LEARN. PLEASE FORGIVE ME.
IT IS NOT A QUESTION OF FORGIVENESS, MY SON. IT IS A QUESTION OF WORTHINESS.
CLEARLY YOU ARE NOT WORTHY OF MJOLNIR AND ALL THAT IT SYMBOLIZES.
PERHAPS THERE EXISTS SOMEONE IN THE NINE WORLDS WHO IS!
AS FOR YOU, THOR...
GO AND MEET YOUR FATE!
FATHER--
NO!

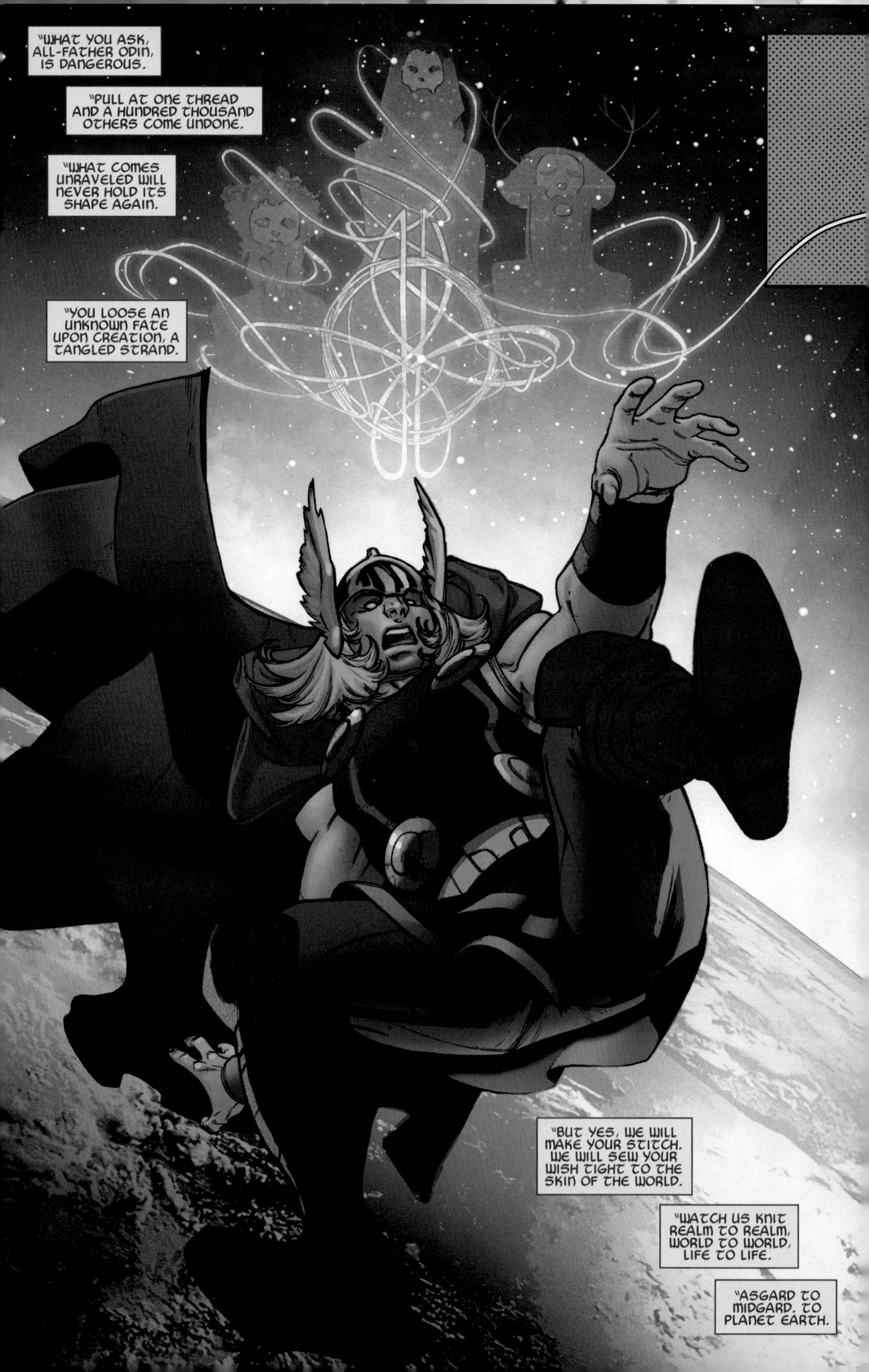
"WHAT YOU ASK, ALL-FATHER ODIN, IS DANGEROUS.
"PULL AT ONE THREAD AND A HUNDRED THOUSAND OTHERS COME UNDONE.
"WHAT COMES UNRAVELED WILL NEVER HOLD ITS SHAPE AGAIN.
"YOU LOOSE AN UNKNOWN FATE UPON CREATION, A TANGLED STRAND.
"BUT YES, WE WILL MAKE YOUR STITCH. WE WILL SEW YOUR WISH TIGHT TO THE SKIN OF THE WORLD.
"WATCH US KNIT REALM TO REALM, WORLD TO WORLD, LIFE TO LIFE.
"ASGARD TO MIDGARD. TO PLANET EARTH.

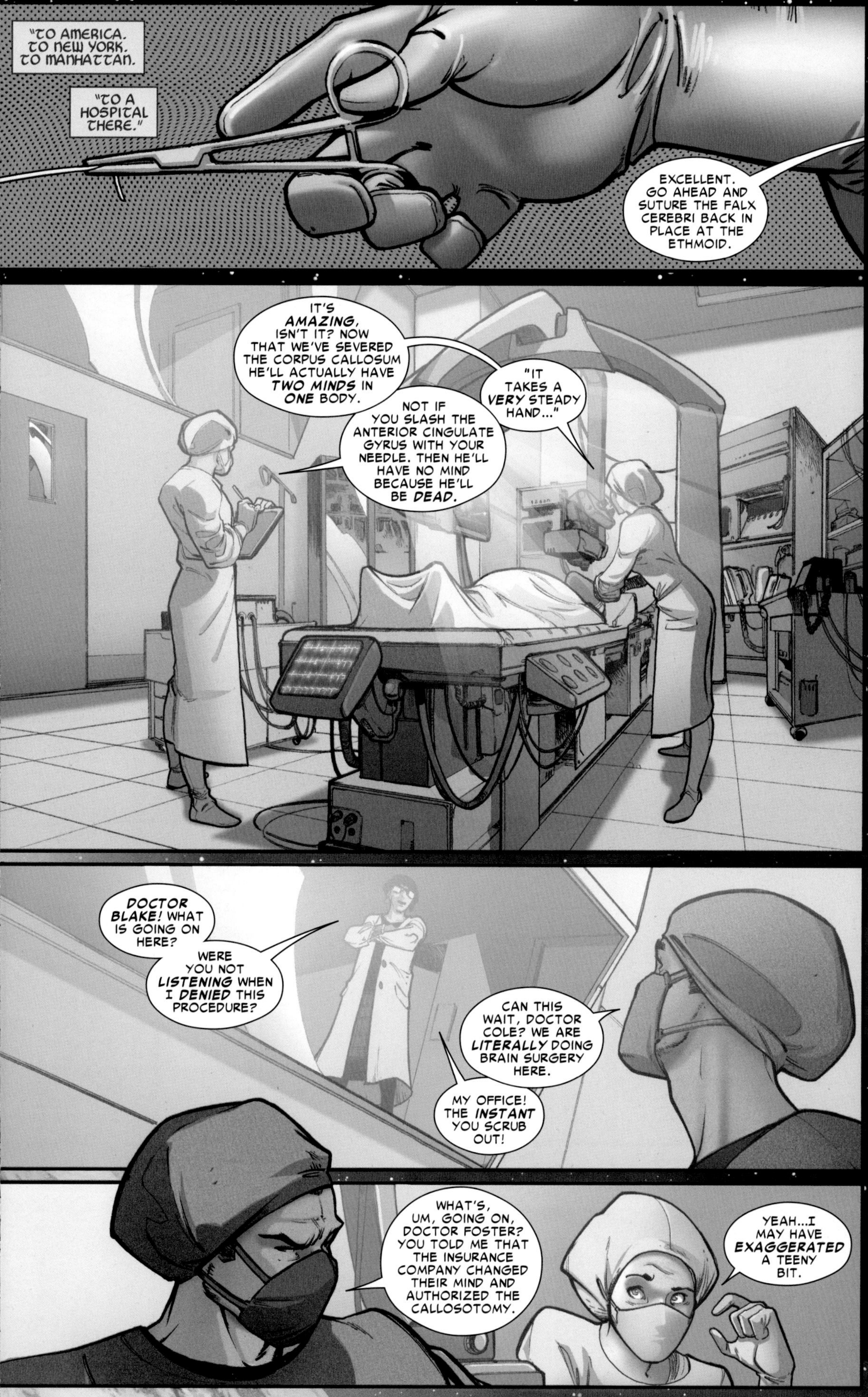
"TO AMERICA. TO NEW YORK. TO MANHATTAN.
"TO A HOSPITAL THERE."
EXCELLENT. GO AHEAD AND SUTURE THE FALX CEREBRI BACK IN PLACE AT THE ETHMOID.
IT'S AMAZING, ISN'T IT? NOW THAT WE'VE SEVERED THE CORPUS CALLOSUM HE'LL ACTUALLY HAVE TWO MINDS IN ONE BODY.
"IT TAKES A VERY STEADY HAND..."
NOT IF YOU SLASH THE ANTERIOR CINGULATE GYRUS WITH YOUR NEEDLE. THEN HE'LL HAVE NO MIND BECAUSE HE'LL BE DEAD.
DOCTOR BLAKE! WHAT IS GOING ON HERE?
WERE YOU NOT LISTENING WHEN I DENIED THIS PROCEDURE?
CAN THIS WAIT, DOCTOR COLE? WE ARE LITERALLY DOING BRAIN SURGERY HERE.
MY OFFICE! THE INSTANT YOU SCRUB OUT!
WHAT'S, UM, GOING ON, DOCTOR FOSTER? YOU TOLD ME THAT THE INSURANCE COMPANY CHANGED THEIR MIND AND AUTHORIZED THE CALLOSOTOMY.
YEAH...I MAY HAVE EXAGGERATED A TEENY BIT.

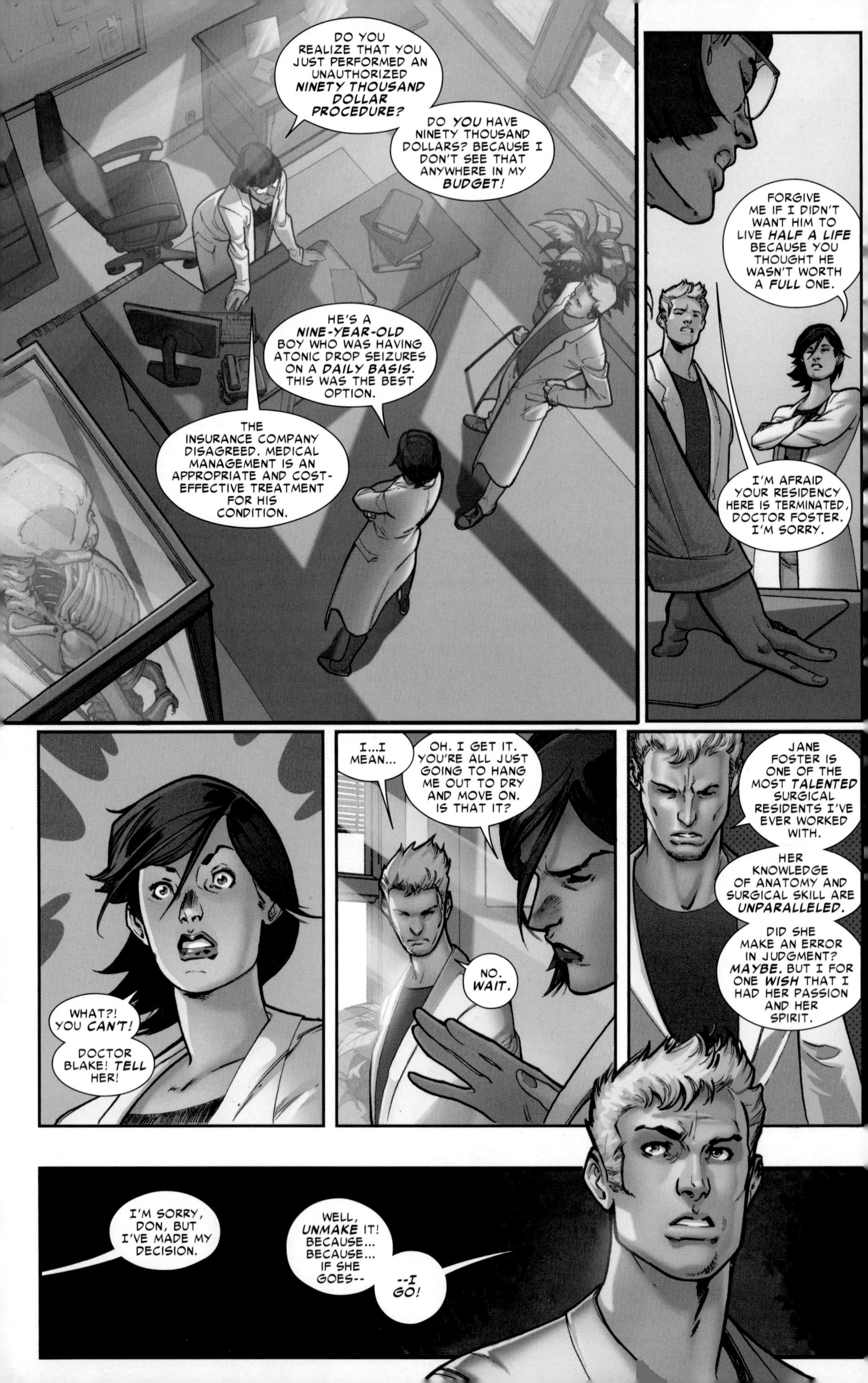
DO YOU REALIZE THAT YOU JUST PERFORMED AN UNAUTHORIZED NINETY THOUSAND DOLLAR PROCEDURE?
DO YOU HAVE NINETY THOUSAND DOLLARS? BECAUSE I DON'T SEE THAT ANYWHERE IN MY BUDGET!
HE'S A NINE-YEAR-OLD BOY WHO WAS HAVING ATONIC DROP SEIZURES ON A DAILY BASIS. THIS WAS THE BEST OPTION.
THE INSURANCE COMPANY DISAGREED. MEDICAL MANAGEMENT IS AN APPROPRIATE AND COST-EFFECTIVE TREATMENT FOR HIS CONDITION.
FORGIVE ME IF I DIDN'T WANT HIM TO LIVE HALF A LIFE BECAUSE YOU THOUGHT HE WASN'T WORTH A FULL ONE.
I'M AFRAID YOUR RESIDENCY HERE IS TERMINATED, DOCTOR FOSTER. I'M SORRY.
WHAT?! YOU CAN'T!
DOCTOR BLAKE! TELL HER!
I...I MEAN...
OH. I GET IT. YOU'RE ALL JUST GOING TO HANG ME OUT TO DRY AND MOVE ON. IS THAT IT?
NO. WAIT.
JANE FOSTER IS ONE OF THE MOST TALENTED SURGICAL RESIDENTS I'VE EVER WORKED WITH.
HER KNOWLEDGE OF ANATOMY AND SURGICAL SKILL ARE UNPARALLELED.
DID SHE MAKE AN ERROR IN JUDGMENT? MAYBE. BUT I FOR ONE WISH THAT I HAD HER PASSION AND HER SPIRIT.
I'M SORRY, DON, BUT I'VE MADE MY DECISION.
WELL, UNMAKE IT! BECAUSE... BECAUSE... IF SHE GOES--
--I GO!

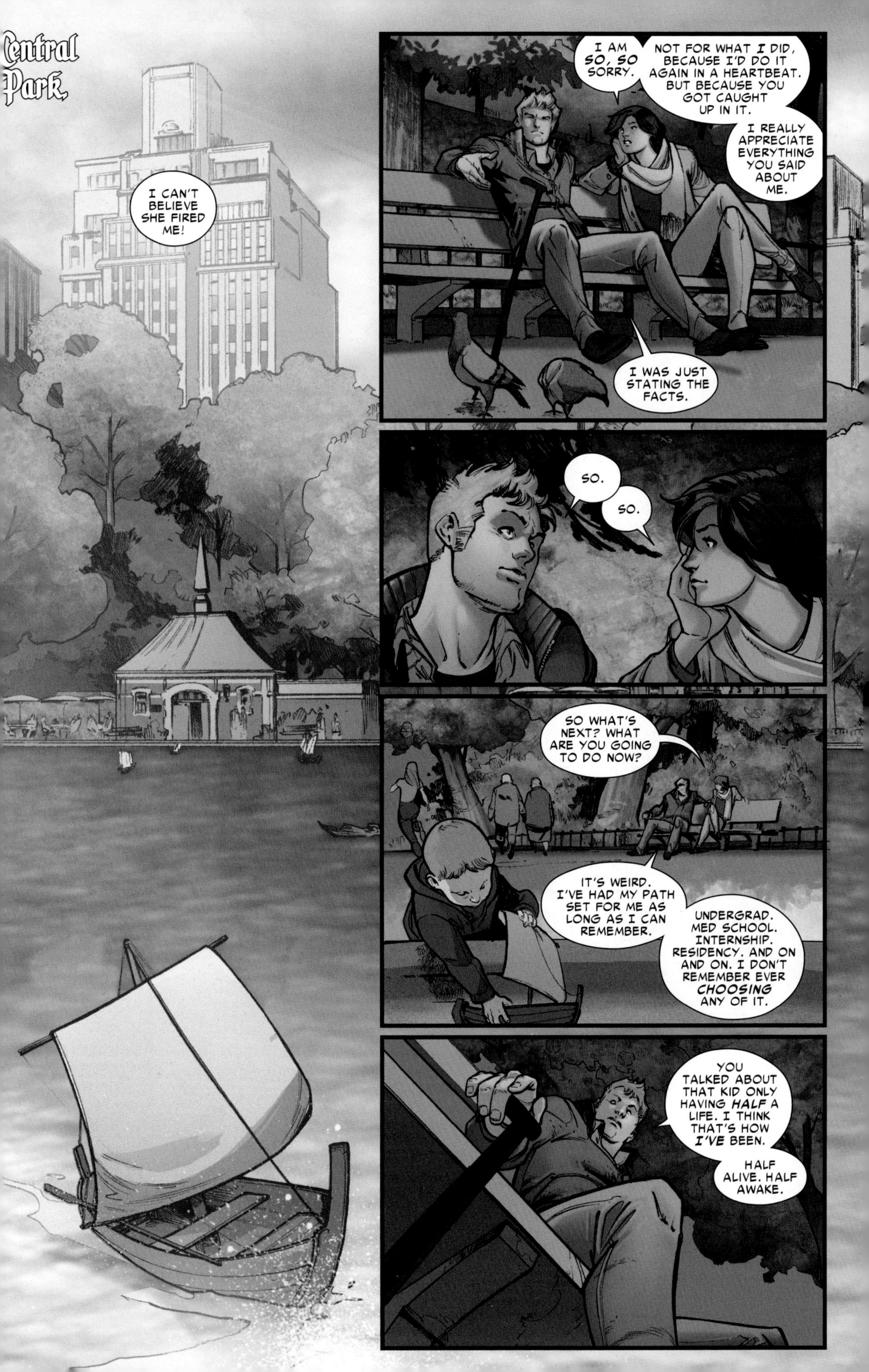
Central Park.
I CAN'T BELIEVE SHE FIRED ME!
I AM SO, SO SORRY.
NOT FOR WHAT I DID, BECAUSE I'D DO IT AGAIN IN A HEARTBEAT. BUT BECAUSE YOU GOT CAUGHT UP IN IT.
I REALLY APPRECIATE EVERYTHING YOU SAID ABOUT ME.
I WAS JUST STATING THE FACTS.
SO.
SO.
SO WHAT'S NEXT? WHAT ARE YOU GOING TO DO NOW?
IT'S WEIRD. I'VE HAD MY PATH SET FOR ME AS LONG AS I CAN REMEMBER.
UNDERGRAD. MED SCHOOL. INTERNSHIP. RESIDENCY. AND ON AND ON. I DON'T REMEMBER EVER CHOOSING ANY OF IT.
YOU TALKED ABOUT THAT KID ONLY HAVING HALF A LIFE. I THINK THAT'S HOW I'VE BEEN.
HALF ALIVE. HALF AWAKE.

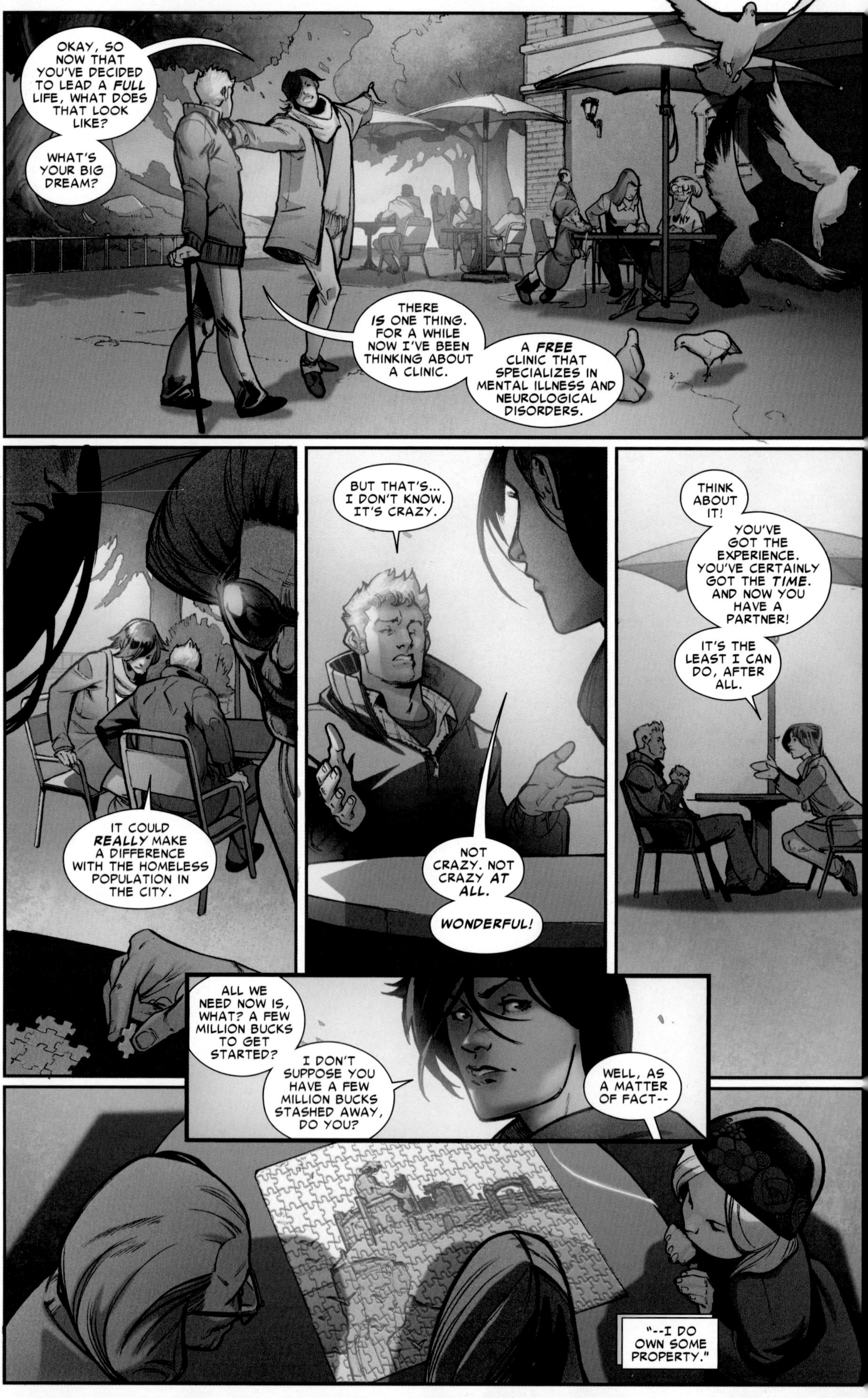
OKAY, SO NOW THAT YOU'VE DECIDED TO LEAD A *FULL* LIFE, WHAT DOES THAT LOOK LIKE?
WHAT'S YOUR BIG DREAM?
THERE *IS* ONE THING. FOR A WHILE NOW I'VE BEEN THINKING ABOUT A CLINIC.
A *FREE* CLINIC THAT SPECIALIZES IN MENTAL ILLNESS AND NEUROLOGICAL DISORDERS.
IT COULD *REALLY* MAKE A DIFFERENCE WITH THE HOMELESS POPULATION IN THE CITY.
BUT THAT'S... I DON'T KNOW. IT'S CRAZY.
NOT CRAZY. NOT CRAZY *AT ALL.*
WONDERFUL!
THINK ABOUT IT!
YOU'VE GOT THE EXPERIENCE. YOU'VE CERTAINLY GOT THE *TIME*. AND NOW YOU HAVE A PARTNER!
IT'S THE LEAST I CAN DO, AFTER ALL.
ALL WE NEED NOW IS, WHAT? A FEW MILLION BUCKS TO GET STARTED?
I DON'T SUPPOSE YOU HAVE A FEW MILLION BUCKS STASHED AWAY, DO YOU?
WELL, AS A MATTER OF FACT--
"--I DO OWN SOME PROPERTY."

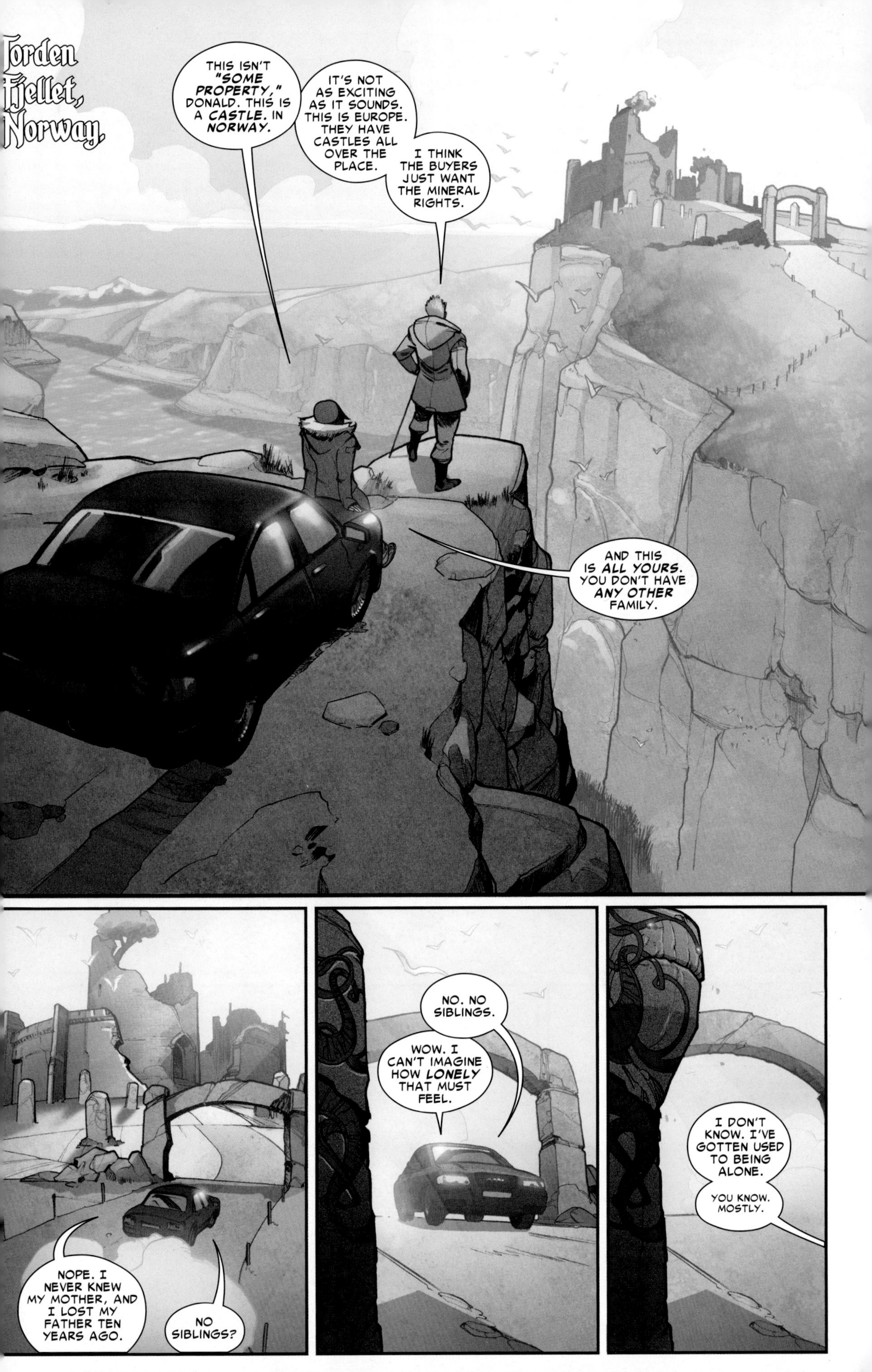
Jorden Fjellet, Norway.
THIS ISN'T "SOME PROPERTY," DONALD. THIS IS A CASTLE. IN NORWAY.
IT'S NOT AS EXCITING AS IT SOUNDS. THIS IS EUROPE. THEY HAVE CASTLES ALL OVER THE PLACE.
I THINK THE BUYERS JUST WANT THE MINERAL RIGHTS.
AND THIS IS ALL YOURS. YOU DON'T HAVE ANY OTHER FAMILY.
NOPE. I NEVER KNEW MY MOTHER, AND I LOST MY FATHER TEN YEARS AGO.
NO SIBLINGS?
NO. NO SIBLINGS.
WOW. I CAN'T IMAGINE HOW LONELY THAT MUST FEEL.
I DON'T KNOW. I'VE GOTTEN USED TO BEING ALONE.
YOU KNOW. MOSTLY.

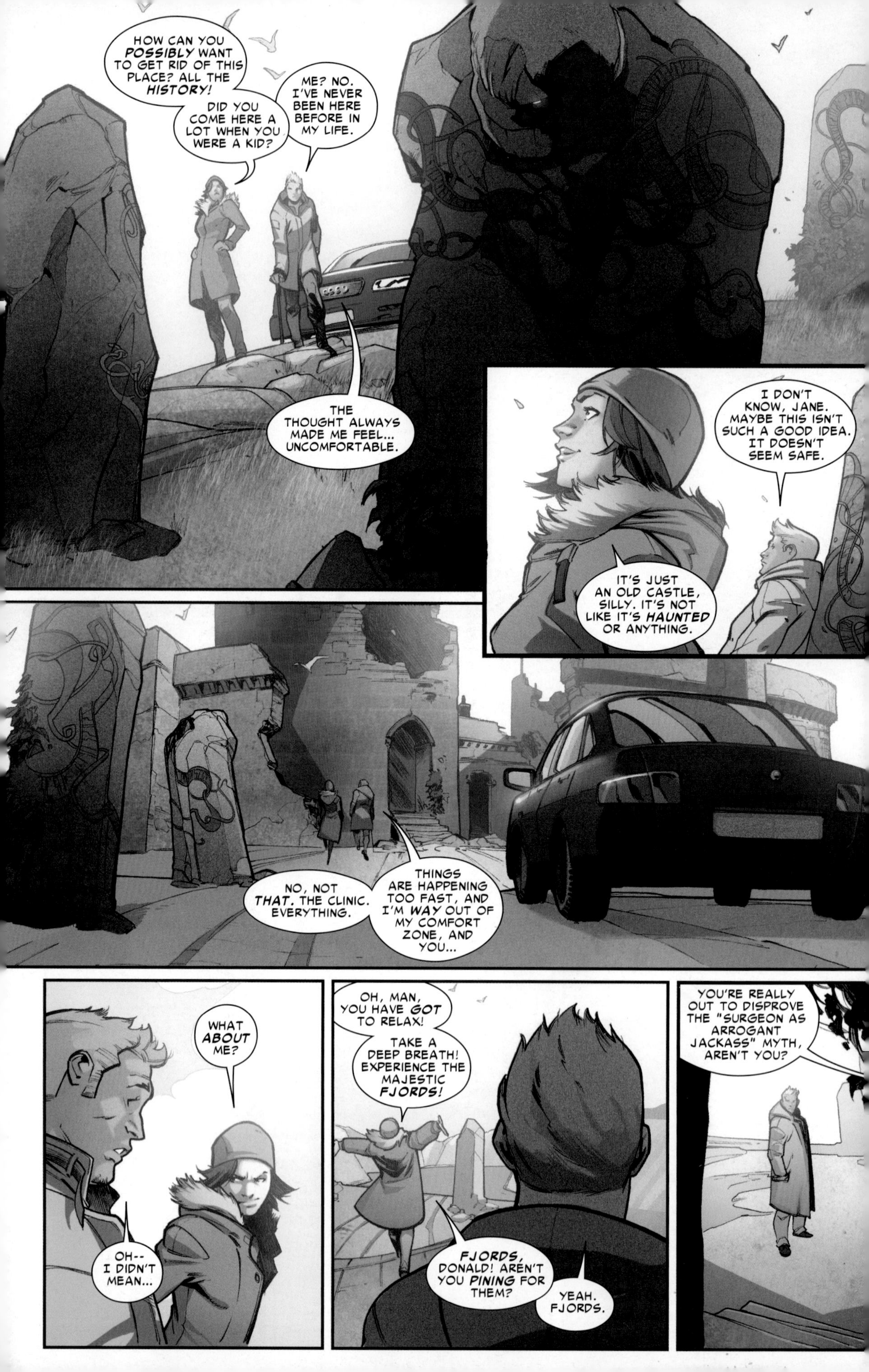
HOW CAN YOU POSSIBLY WANT TO GET RID OF THIS PLACE? ALL THE HISTORY!
DID YOU COME HERE A LOT WHEN YOU WERE A KID?
ME? NO. I'VE NEVER BEEN HERE BEFORE IN MY LIFE.
THE THOUGHT ALWAYS MADE ME FEEL... UNCOMFORTABLE.
I DON'T KNOW, JANE. MAYBE THIS ISN'T SUCH A GOOD IDEA. IT DOESN'T SEEM SAFE.
IT'S JUST AN OLD CASTLE, SILLY. IT'S NOT LIKE IT'S HAUNTED OR ANYTHING.
NO, NOT THAT. THE CLINIC. EVERYTHING.
THINGS ARE HAPPENING TOO FAST, AND I'M WAY OUT OF MY COMFORT ZONE, AND YOU...
WHAT ABOUT ME?
OH-- I DIDN'T MEAN...
OH, MAN, YOU HAVE GOT TO RELAX!
TAKE A DEEP BREATH! EXPERIENCE THE MAJESTIC FJORDS!
FJORDS, DONALD! AREN'T YOU PINING FOR THEM?
YEAH. FJORDS.
YOU'RE REALLY OUT TO DISPROVE THE "SURGEON AS ARROGANT JACKASS" MYTH, AREN'T YOU?

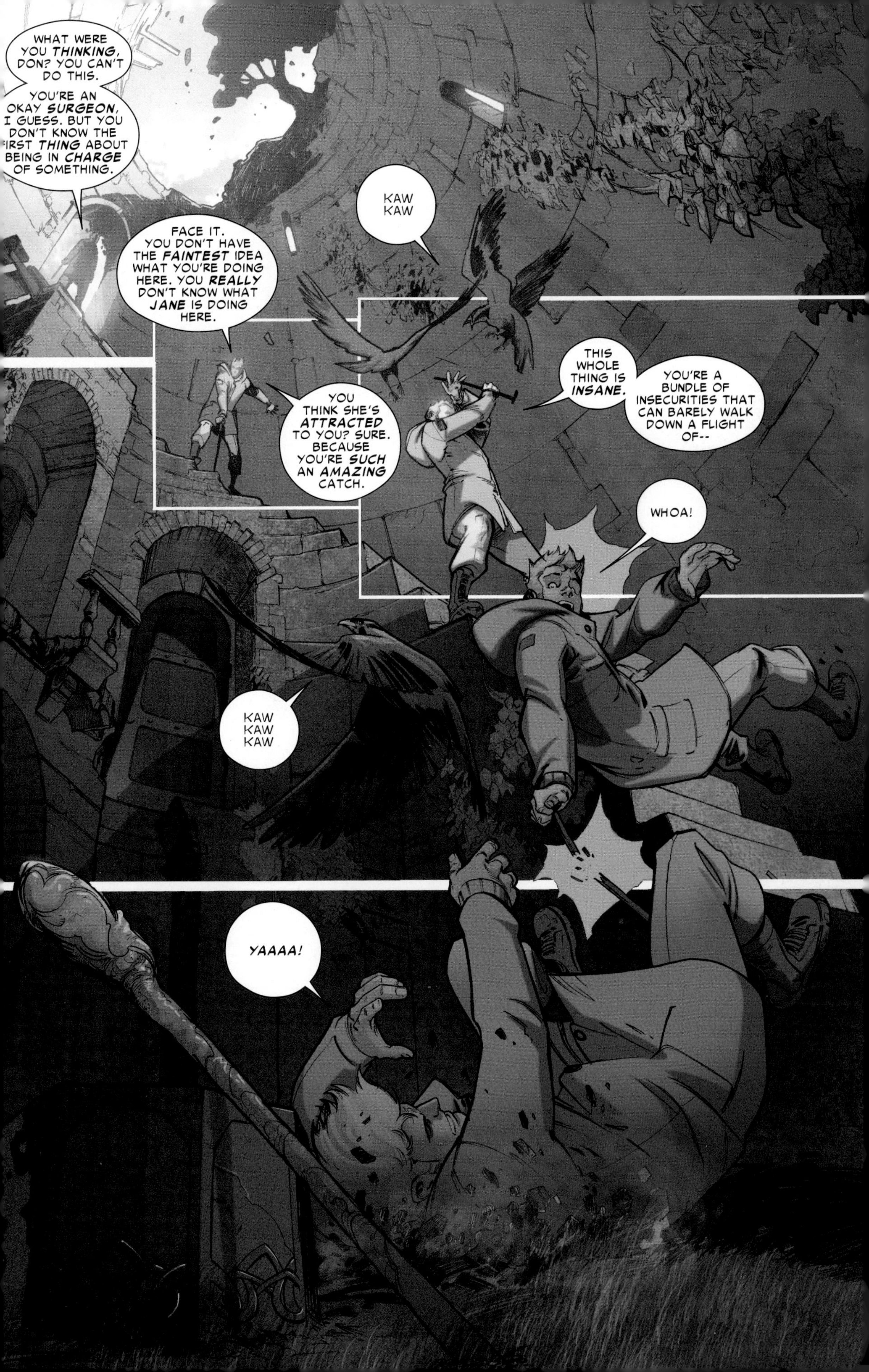
WHAT WERE YOU *THINKING*, DON? YOU CAN'T DO THIS.
YOU'RE AN OKAY *SURGEON*, I GUESS. BUT YOU DON'T KNOW THE FIRST *THING* ABOUT BEING IN *CHARGE* OF SOMETHING.
KAW KAW
FACE IT. YOU DON'T HAVE THE *FAINTEST* IDEA WHAT YOU'RE DOING HERE. YOU *REALLY* DON'T KNOW WHAT *JANE* IS DOING HERE.
YOU THINK SHE'S *ATTRACTED* TO YOU? SURE. BECAUSE YOU'RE *SUCH* AN *AMAZING* CATCH.
THIS WHOLE THING IS *INSANE.*
YOU'RE A BUNDLE OF INSECURITIES THAT CAN BARELY WALK DOWN A FLIGHT OF--
WHOA!
KAW KAW KAW
YAAAA!

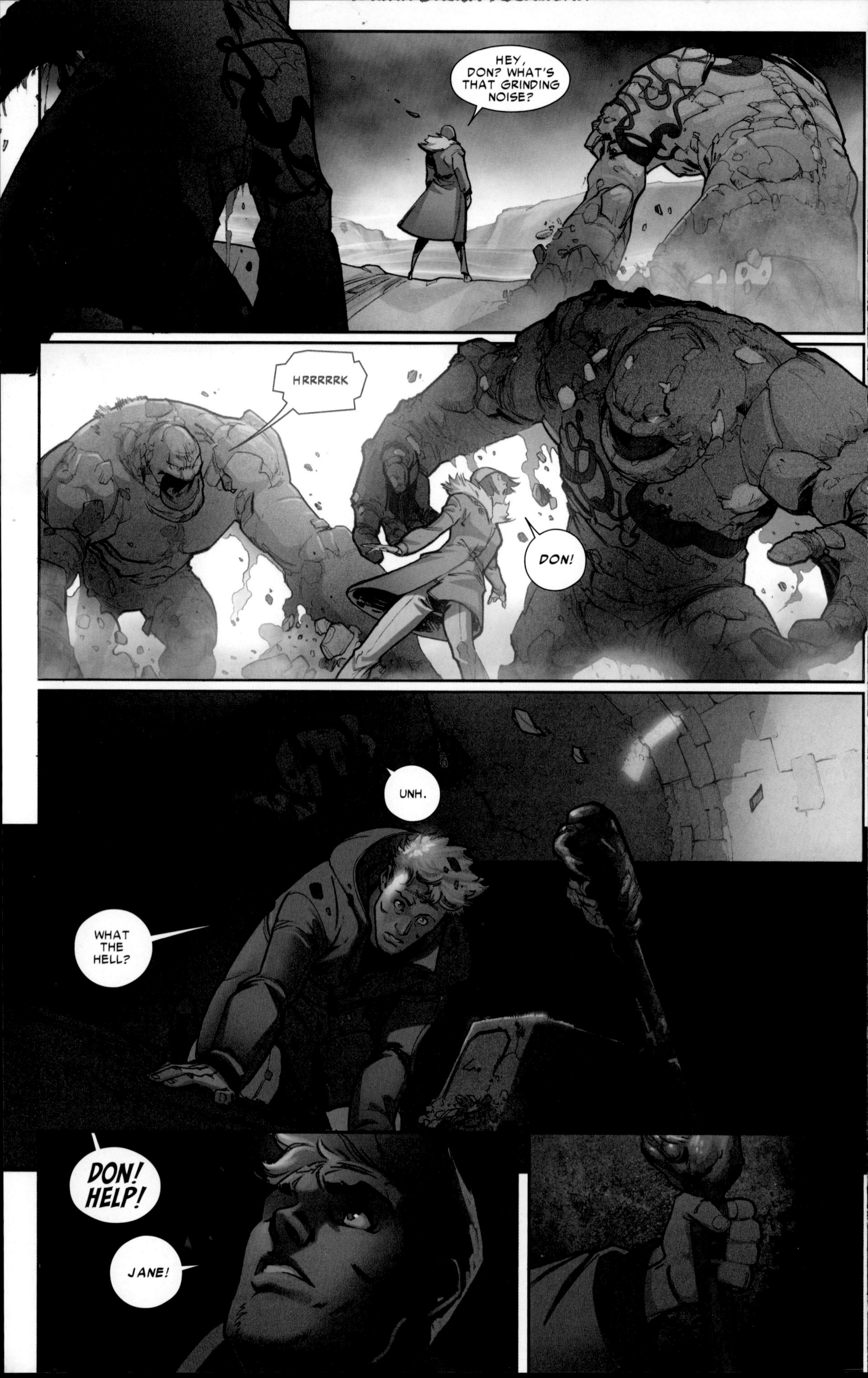
HEY, DON? WHAT'S THAT GRINDING NOISE?
HRRRRRK
DON!
UNH.
WHAT THE HELL?
DON! HELP!
JANE!

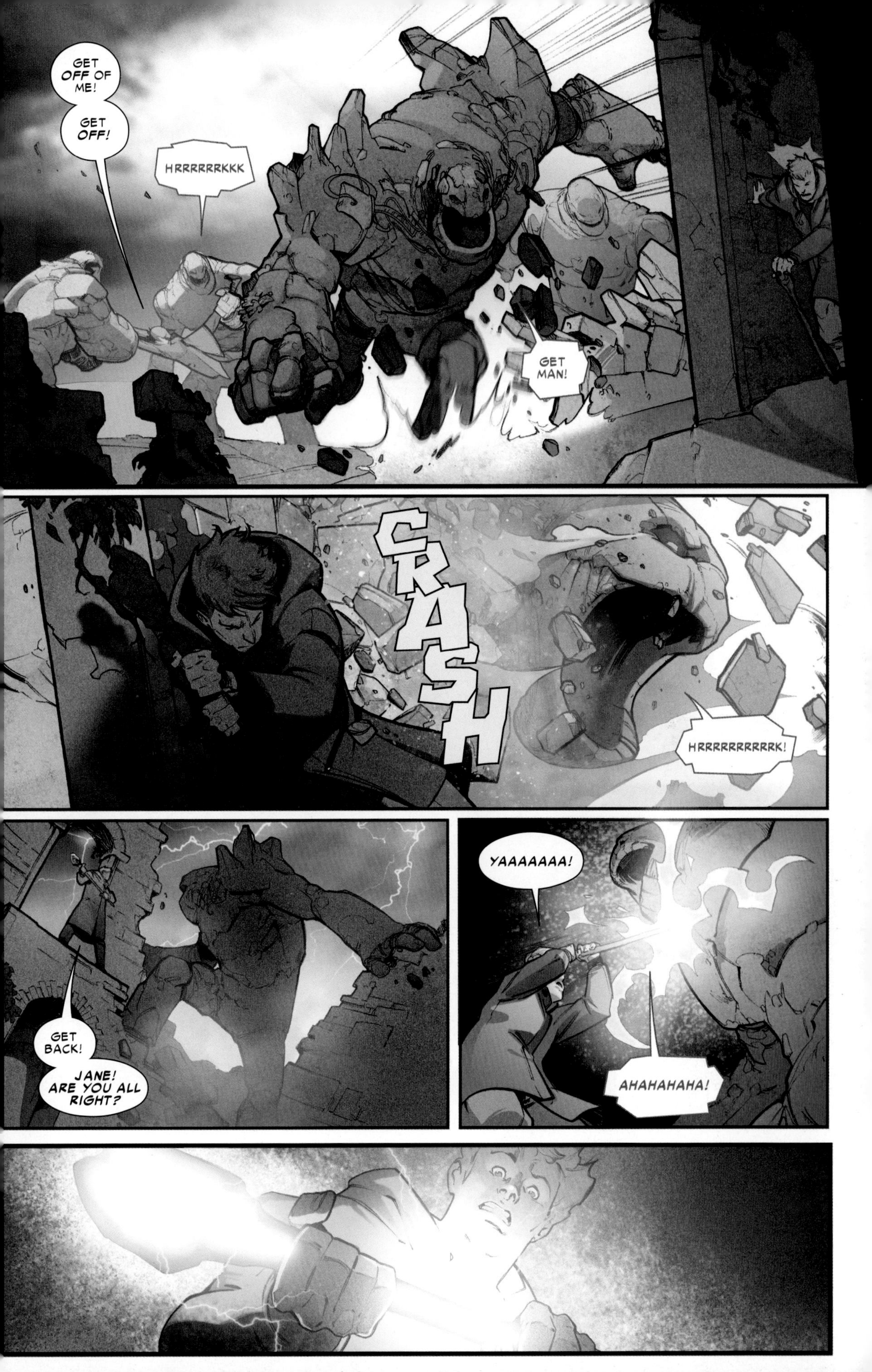
GET OFF OF ME!
GET OFF!
HRRRRRRKKK
GET MAN!
CRASH
HRRRRRRRRRK!
GET BACK!
JANE! ARE YOU ALL RIGHT?
YAAAAAAA!
AHAHAHAHA!

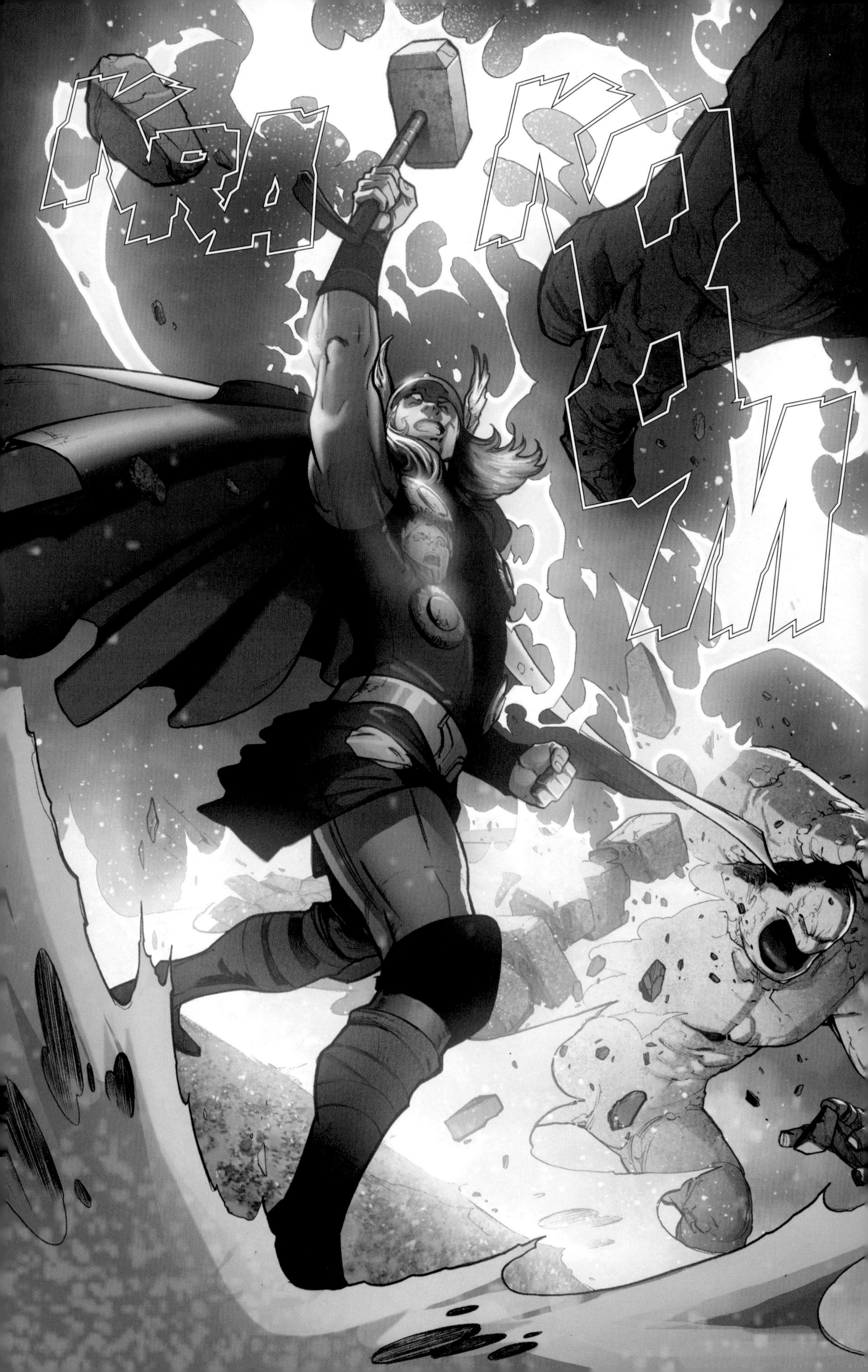
KRA KOOM

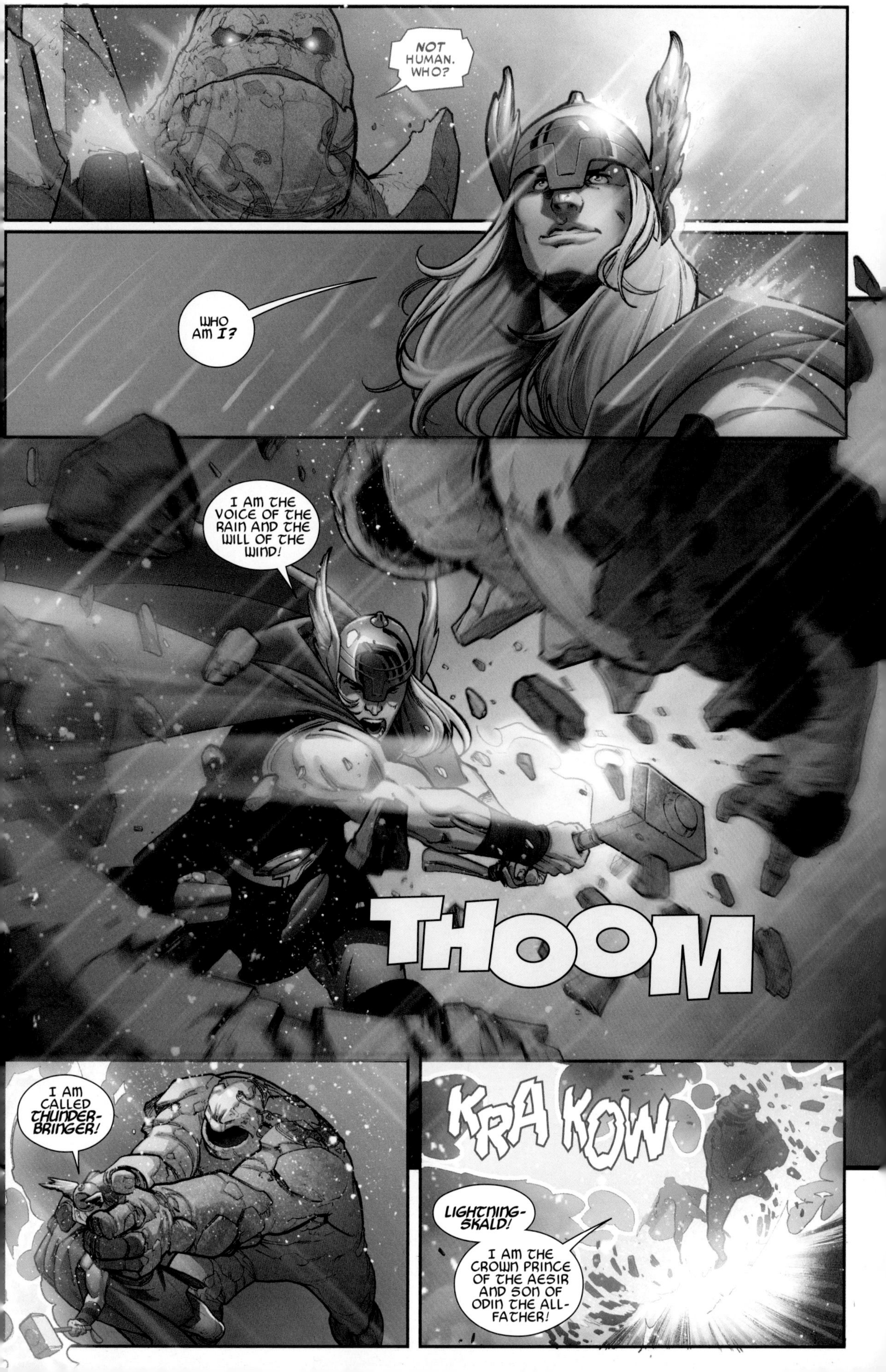
NOT HUMAN. WHO?
WHO AM I?
I AM THE VOICE OF THE RAIN AND THE WILL OF THE WIND!
THOOM
I AM CALLED THUNDER-BRINGER!
KRA KOW
LIGHTNING-SKALD!
I AM THE CROWN PRINCE OF THE AESIR AND SON OF ODIN THE ALL-FATHER!

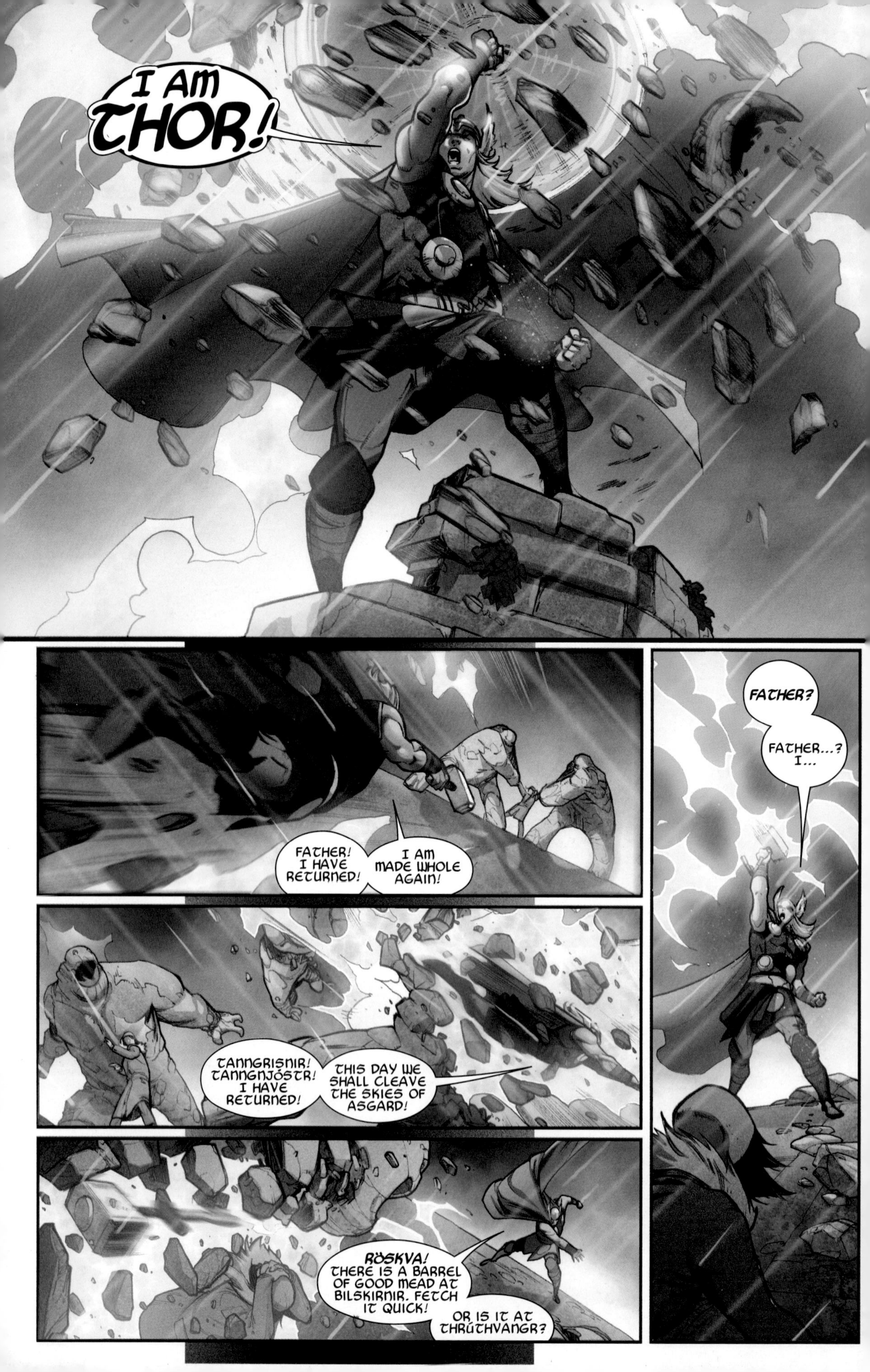

I AM THOR!
FATHER! I HAVE RETURNED!
I AM MADE WHOLE AGAIN!
TANNGRISNIR! TANNGNJÓSTR! I HAVE RETURNED!
THIS DAY WE SHALL CLEAVE THE SKIES OF ASGARD!
RÖSKVA! THERE IS A BARREL OF GOOD MEAD AT BILSKIRNIR. FETCH IT QUICK!
OR IS IT AT THRÚTHVANGR?
FATHER?
FATHER...? I...

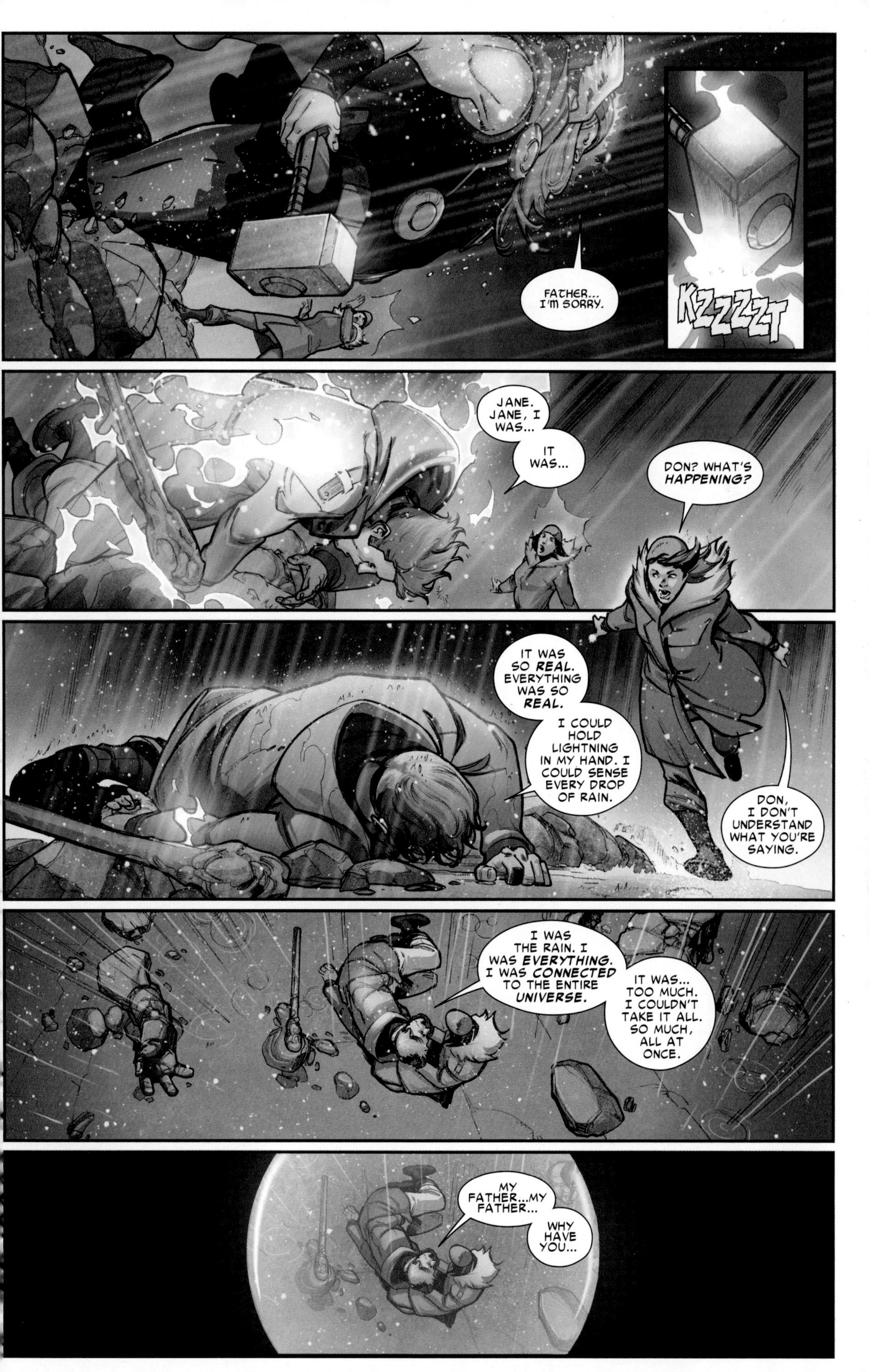

FATHER... I'M SORRY.
KZZZZZT
JANE. JANE, I WAS...
IT WAS...
DON? WHAT'S HAPPENING?
IT WAS SO REAL. EVERYTHING WAS SO REAL.
I COULD HOLD LIGHTNING IN MY HAND. I COULD SENSE EVERY DROP OF RAIN.
DON, I DON'T UNDERSTAND WHAT YOU'RE SAYING.
I WAS THE RAIN. I WAS EVERYTHING. I WAS CONNECTED TO THE ENTIRE UNIVERSE.
IT WAS... TOO MUCH. I COULDN'T TAKE IT ALL. SO MUCH, ALL AT ONCE.
MY FATHER...MY FATHER...
WHY HAVE YOU...

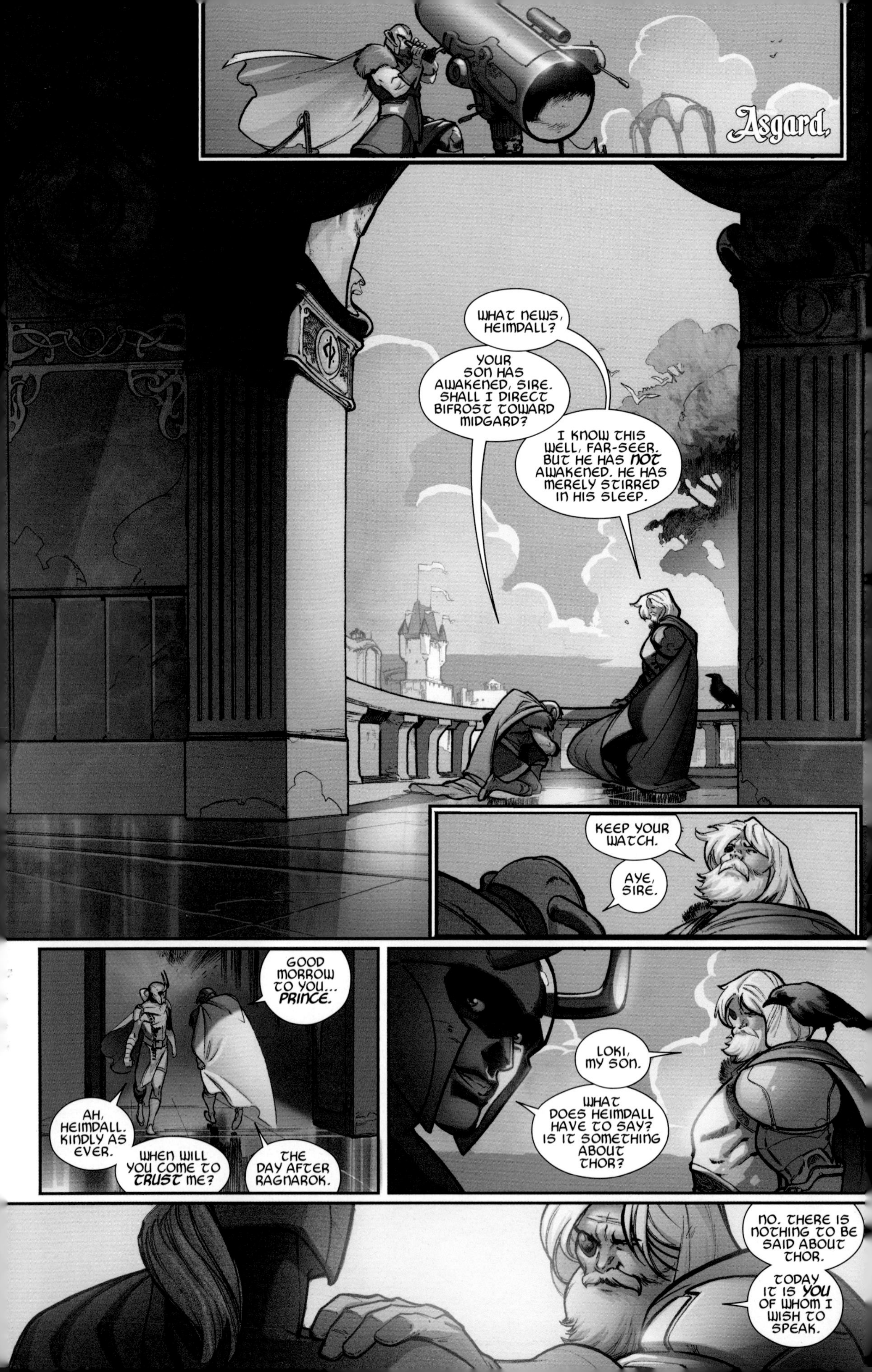
Asgard,
WHAT NEWS, HEIMDALL?
YOUR SON HAS AWAKENED, SIRE. SHALL I DIRECT BIFROST TOWARD MIDGARD?
I KNOW THIS WELL, FAR-SEER. BUT HE HAS NOT AWAKENED. HE HAS MERELY STIRRED IN HIS SLEEP.
KEEP YOUR WATCH.
AYE, SIRE.
GOOD MORROW TO YOU... PRINCE.
AH, HEIMDALL. KINDLY AS EVER.
WHEN WILL YOU COME TO TRUST ME?
THE DAY AFTER RAGNAROK.
LOKI, MY SON.
WHAT DOES HEIMDALL HAVE TO SAY? IS IT SOMETHING ABOUT THOR?
NO. THERE IS NOTHING TO BE SAID ABOUT THOR.
TODAY IT IS YOU OF WHOM I WISH TO SPEAK.

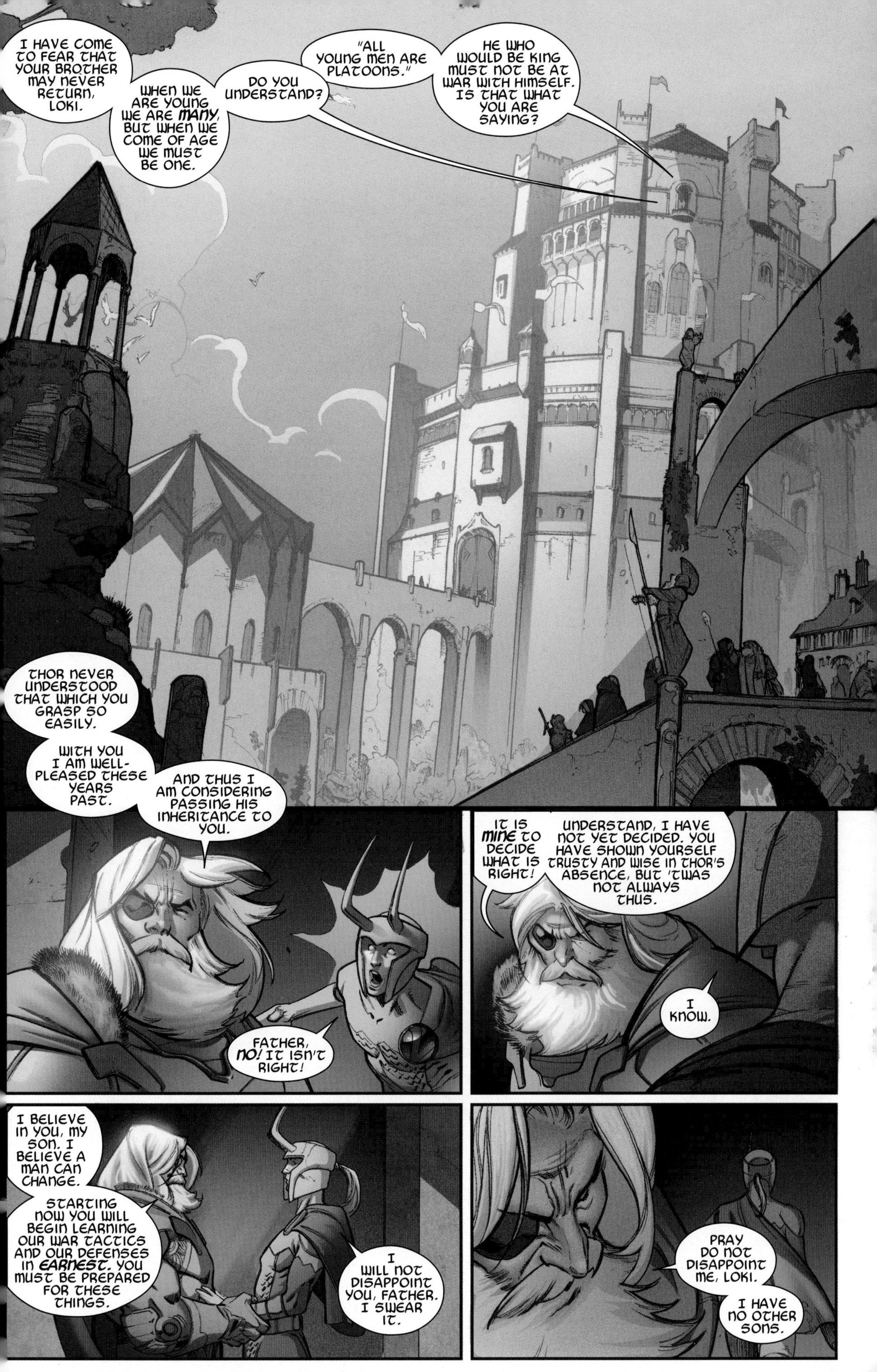
I HAVE COME TO FEAR THAT YOUR BROTHER MAY NEVER RETURN, LOKI.
WHEN WE ARE YOUNG WE ARE MANY, BUT WHEN WE COME OF AGE WE MUST BE ONE.
DO YOU UNDERSTAND?
"ALL YOUNG MEN ARE PLATOONS."
HE WHO WOULD BE KING MUST NOT BE AT WAR WITH HIMSELF. IS THAT WHAT YOU ARE SAYING?
THOR NEVER UNDERSTOOD THAT WHICH YOU GRASP SO EASILY.
WITH YOU I AM WELL-PLEASED THESE YEARS PAST.
AND THUS I AM CONSIDERING PASSING HIS INHERITANCE TO YOU.
FATHER, NO! IT ISN'T RIGHT!
IT IS MINE TO DECIDE WHAT IS RIGHT!
UNDERSTAND, I HAVE NOT YET DECIDED. YOU HAVE SHOWN YOURSELF TRUSTY AND WISE IN THOR'S ABSENCE, BUT 'TWAS NOT ALWAYS THUS.
I KNOW.
I BELIEVE IN YOU, MY SON. I BELIEVE A MAN CAN CHANGE.
STARTING NOW YOU WILL BEGIN LEARNING OUR WAR TACTICS AND OUR DEFENSES IN EARNEST. YOU MUST BE PREPARED FOR THESE THINGS.
I WILL NOT DISAPPOINT YOU, FATHER. I SWEAR IT.
PRAY DO NOT DISAPPOINT ME, LOKI.
I HAVE NO OTHER SONS.

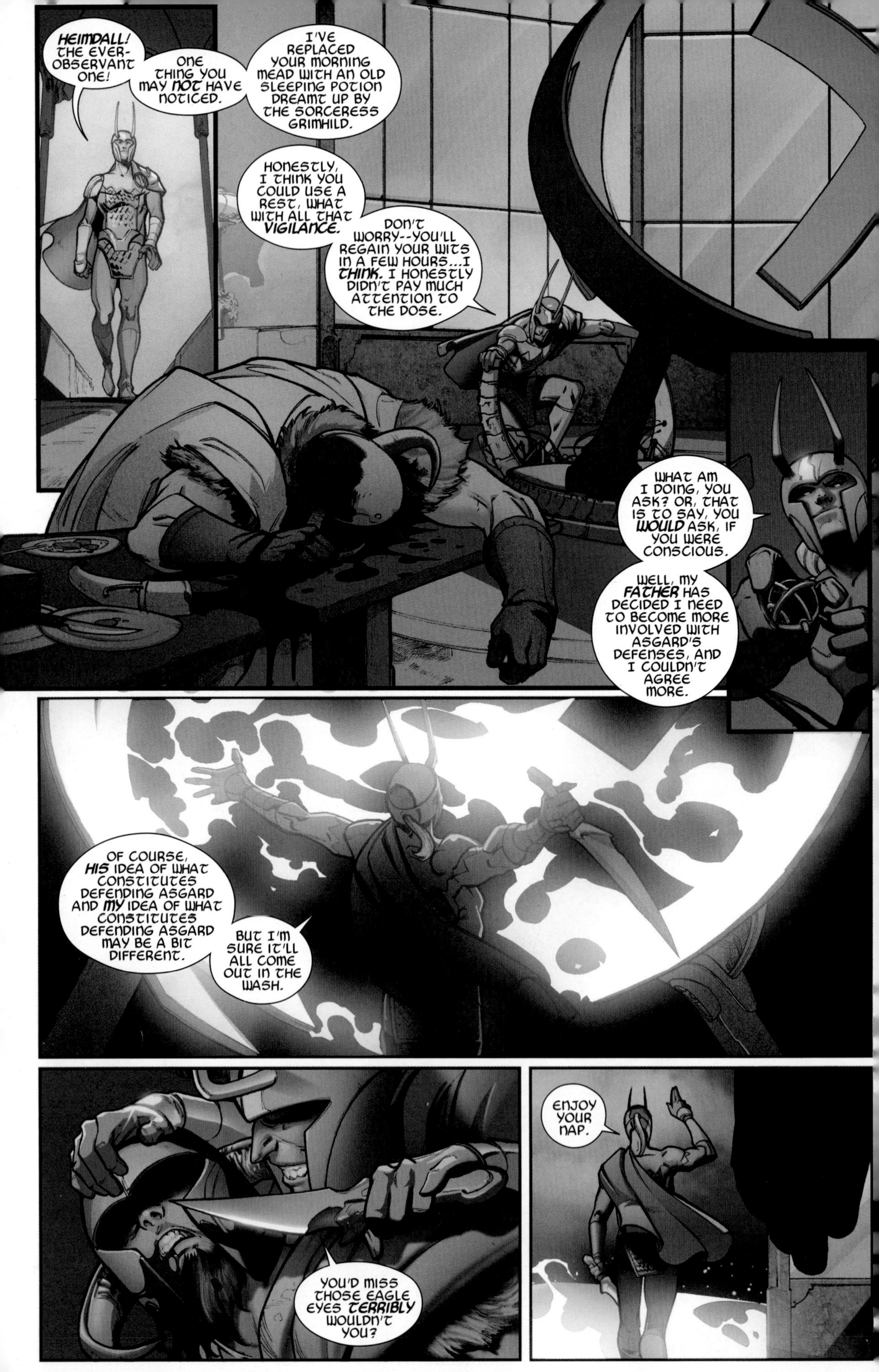
HEIMDALL! THE EVER-OBSERVANT ONE!
ONE THING YOU MAY NOT HAVE NOTICED.
I'VE REPLACED YOUR MORNING MEAD WITH AN OLD SLEEPING POTION DREAMT UP BY THE SORCERESS GRIMHILD.
HONESTLY, I THINK YOU COULD USE A REST, WHAT WITH ALL THAT VIGILANCE.
DON'T WORRY--YOU'LL REGAIN YOUR WITS IN A FEW HOURS...I THINK. I HONESTLY DIDN'T PAY MUCH ATTENTION TO THE DOSE.
WHAT AM I DOING, YOU ASK? OR, THAT IS TO SAY, YOU WOULD ASK, IF YOU WERE CONSCIOUS.
WELL, MY FATHER HAS DECIDED I NEED TO BECOME MORE INVOLVED WITH ASGARD'S DEFENSES, AND I COULDN'T AGREE MORE.
OF COURSE, HIS IDEA OF WHAT CONSTITUTES DEFENDING ASGARD AND MY IDEA OF WHAT CONSTITUTES DEFENDING ASGARD MAY BE A BIT DIFFERENT.
BUT I'M SURE IT'LL ALL COME OUT IN THE WASH.
YOU'D MISS THOSE EAGLE EYES TERRIBLY WOULDN'T YOU?
ENJOY YOUR NAP.

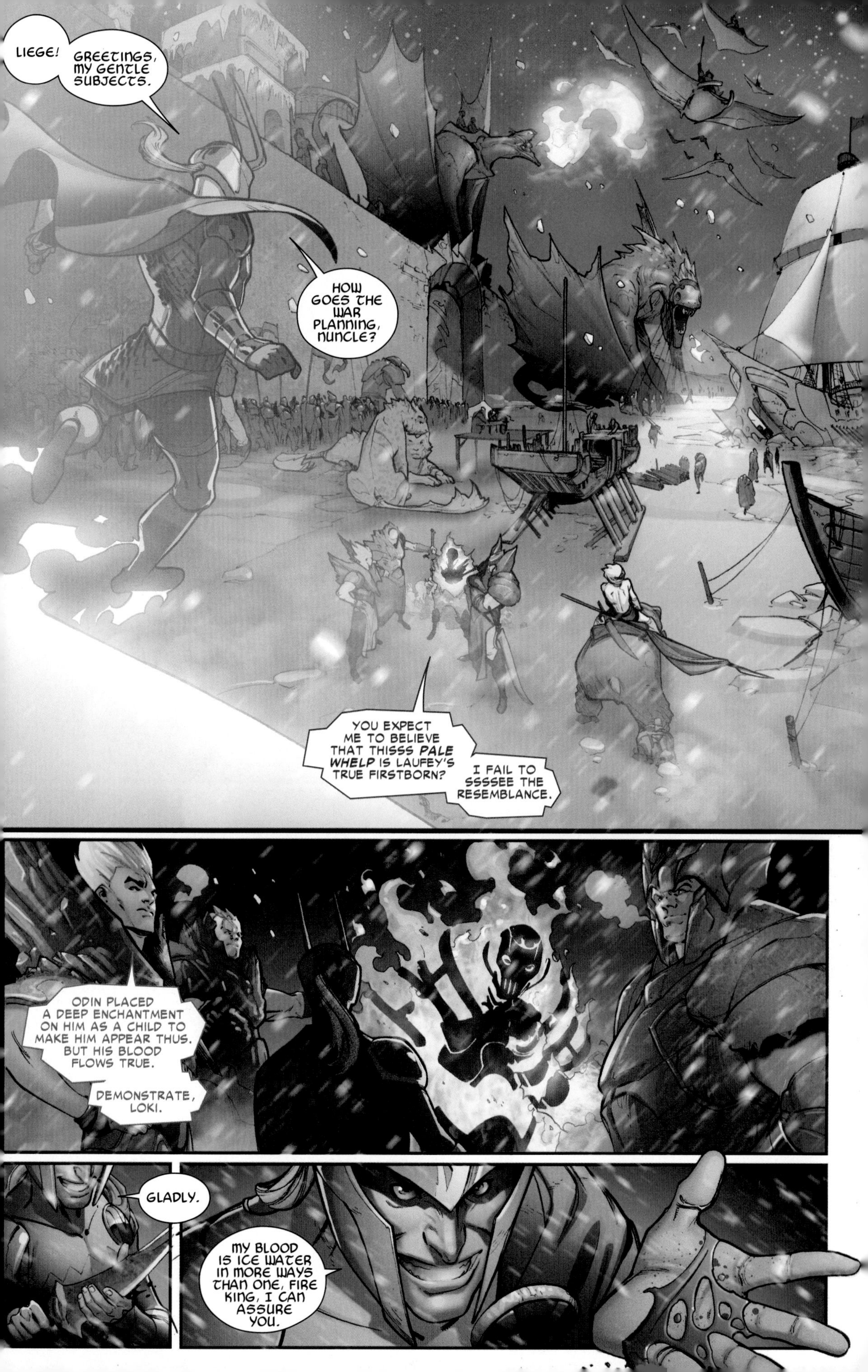
LIEGE!
GREETINGS, MY GENTLE SUBJECTS.
HOW GOES THE WAR PLANNING, NUNCLE?
YOU EXPECT ME TO BELIEVE THAT THISSS PALE WHELP IS LAUFEY'S TRUE FIRSTBORN?
I FAIL TO SSSSEE THE RESEMBLANCE.
ODIN PLACED A DEEP ENCHANTMENT ON HIM AS A CHILD TO MAKE HIM APPEAR THUS. BUT HIS BLOOD FLOWS TRUE.
DEMONSTRATE, LOKI.
GLADLY.
MY BLOOD IS ICE WATER IN MORE WAYS THAN ONE, FIRE KING, I CAN ASSURE YOU.

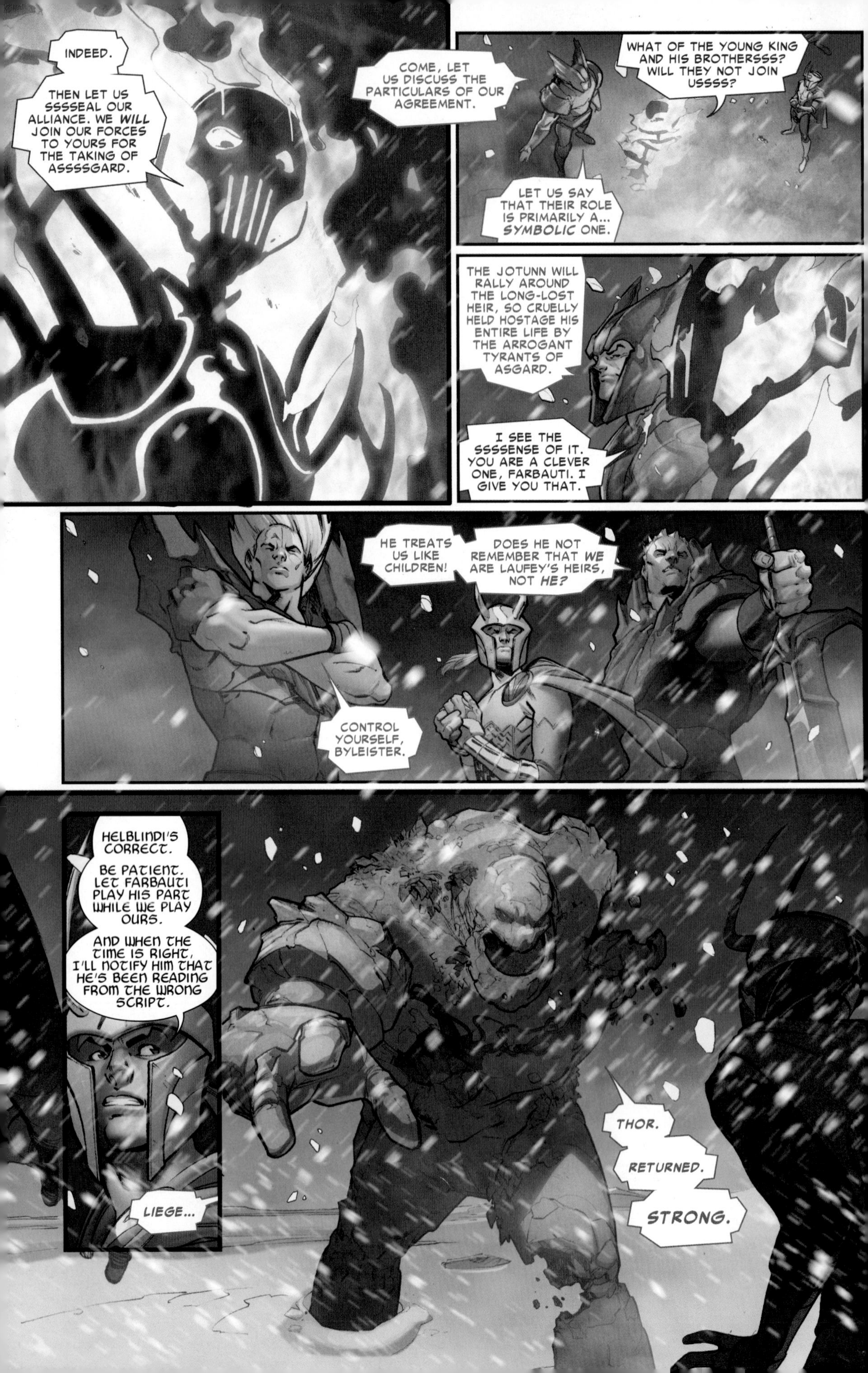
INDEED.
THEN LET US SSSSEAL OUR ALLIANCE. WE WILL JOIN OUR FORCES TO YOURS FOR THE TAKING OF ASSSSGARD.
COME, LET US DISCUSS THE PARTICULARS OF OUR AGREEMENT.
WHAT OF THE YOUNG KING AND HIS BROTHERSSS? WILL THEY NOT JOIN USSSS?
LET US SAY THAT THEIR ROLE IS PRIMARILY A... SYMBOLIC ONE.
THE JOTUNN WILL RALLY AROUND THE LONG-LOST HEIR, SO CRUELLY HELD HOSTAGE HIS ENTIRE LIFE BY THE ARROGANT TYRANTS OF ASGARD.
I SEE THE SSSSENSE OF IT. YOU ARE A CLEVER ONE, FARBAUTI. I GIVE YOU THAT.
HE TREATS US LIKE CHILDREN!
DOES HE NOT REMEMBER THAT WE ARE LAUFEY'S HEIRS, NOT HE?
CONTROL YOURSELF, BYLEISTER.
HELBLINDI'S CORRECT.
BE PATIENT. LET FARBAUTI PLAY HIS PART WHILE WE PLAY OURS.
AND WHEN THE TIME IS RIGHT, I'LL NOTIFY HIM THAT HE'S BEEN READING FROM THE WRONG SCRIPT.
LIEGE...
THOR.
RETURNED.
STRONG.

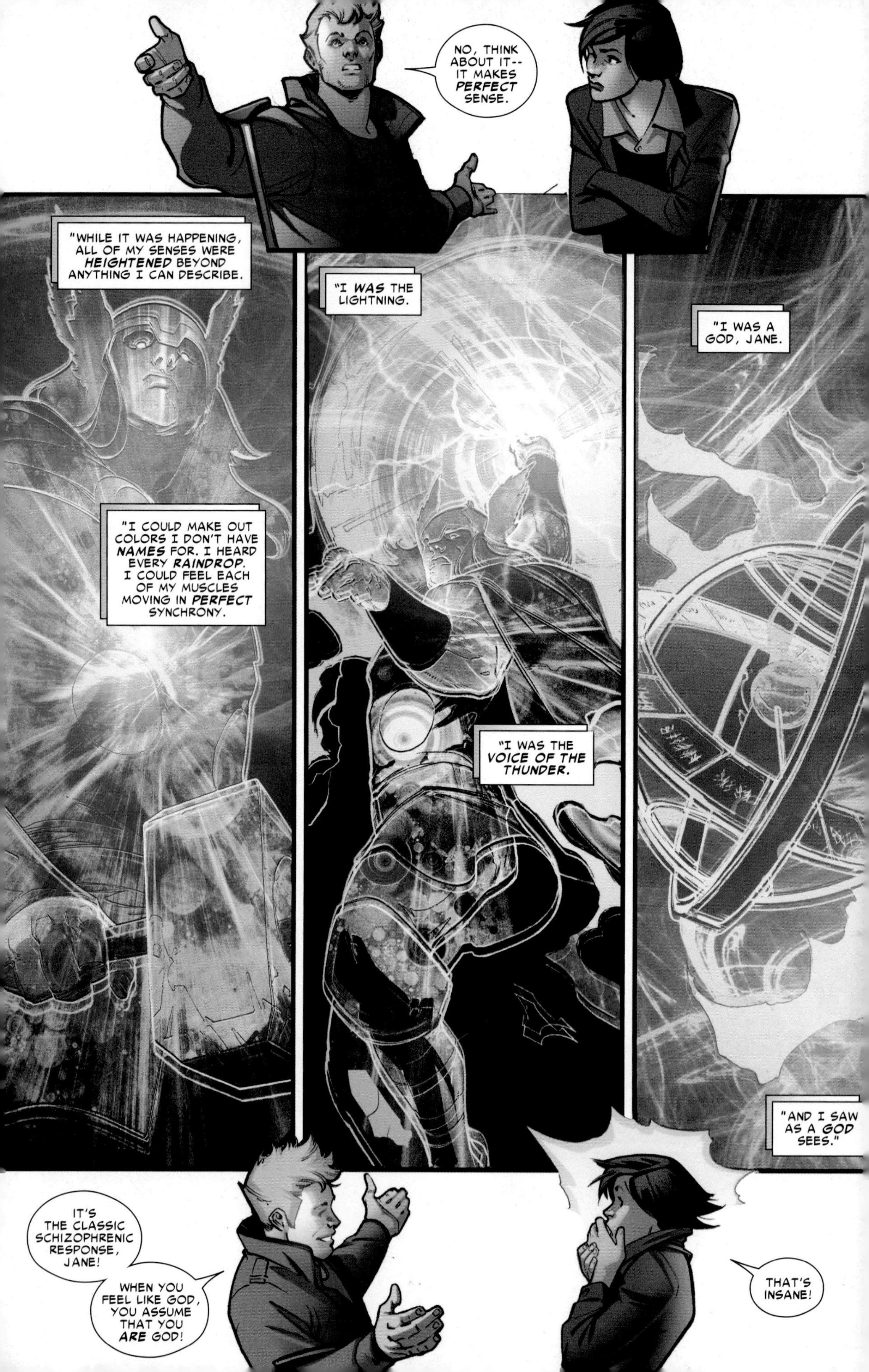
NO, THINK ABOUT IT-- IT MAKES PERFECT SENSE.
"WHILE IT WAS HAPPENING, ALL OF MY SENSES WERE HEIGHTENED BEYOND ANYTHING I CAN DESCRIBE.
"I COULD MAKE OUT COLORS I DON'T HAVE NAMES FOR. I HEARD EVERY RAINDROP. I COULD FEEL EACH OF MY MUSCLES MOVING IN PERFECT SYNCHRONY.
"I WAS THE LIGHTNING.
"I WAS THE VOICE OF THE THUNDER.
"I WAS A GOD, JANE.
"AND I SAW AS A GOD SEES."
IT'S THE CLASSIC SCHIZOPHRENIC RESPONSE, JANE!
WHEN YOU FEEL LIKE GOD, YOU ASSUME THAT YOU ARE GOD!
THAT'S INSANE!

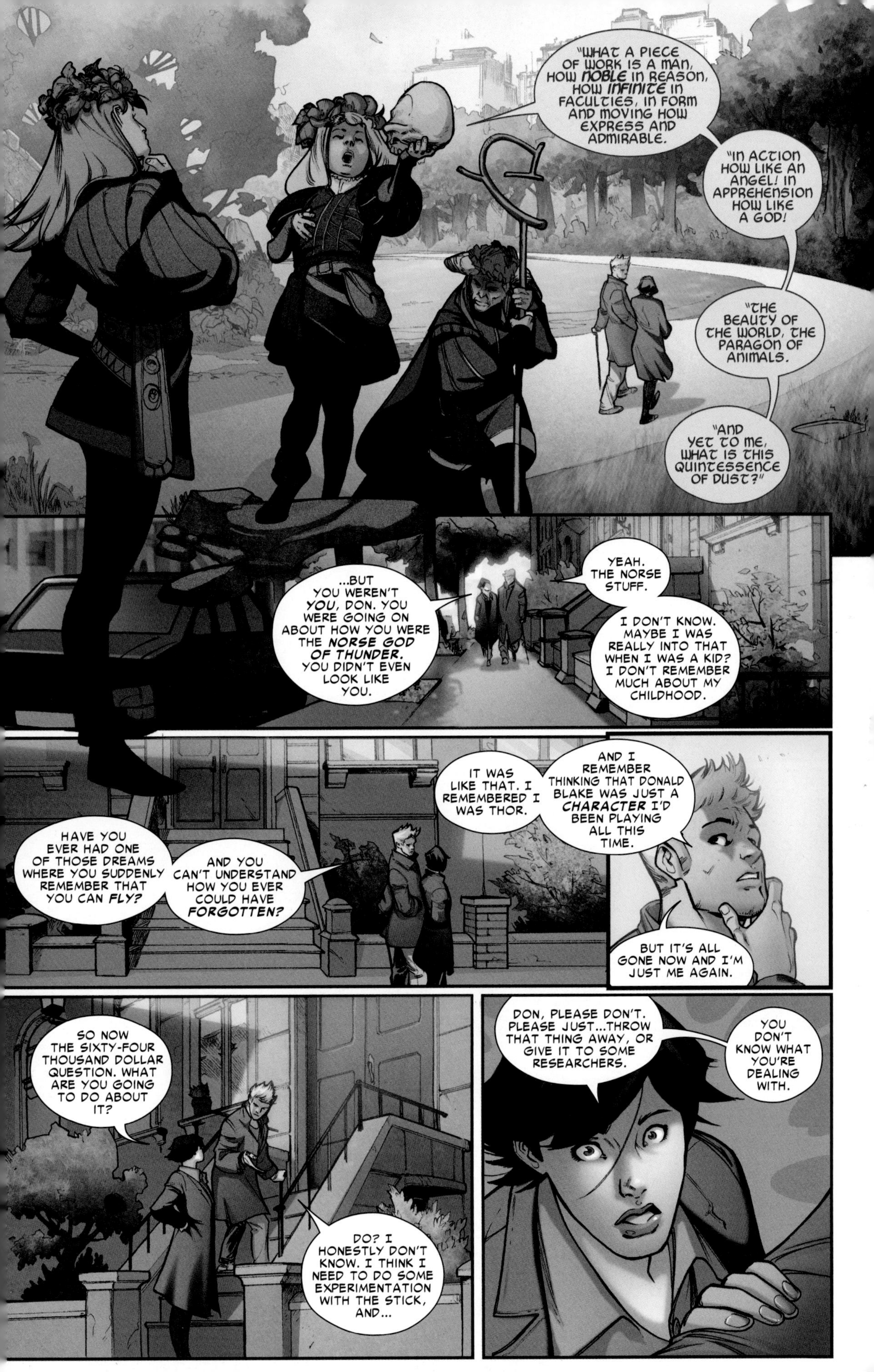
"WHAT A PIECE OF WORK IS A MAN, HOW NOBLE IN REASON, HOW INFINITE IN FACULTIES, IN FORM AND MOVING HOW EXPRESS AND ADMIRABLE.
"IN ACTION HOW LIKE AN ANGEL! IN APPREHENSION HOW LIKE A GOD!
"THE BEAUTY OF THE WORLD, THE PARAGON OF ANIMALS.
"AND YET TO ME, WHAT IS THIS QUINTESSENCE OF DUST?"
...BUT YOU WEREN'T YOU, DON. YOU WERE GOING ON ABOUT HOW YOU WERE THE NORSE GOD OF THUNDER. YOU DIDN'T EVEN LOOK LIKE YOU.
YEAH. THE NORSE STUFF.
I DON'T KNOW. MAYBE I WAS REALLY INTO THAT WHEN I WAS A KID? I DON'T REMEMBER MUCH ABOUT MY CHILDHOOD.
HAVE YOU EVER HAD ONE OF THOSE DREAMS WHERE YOU SUDDENLY REMEMBER THAT YOU CAN FLY?
AND YOU CAN'T UNDERSTAND HOW YOU EVER COULD HAVE FORGOTTEN?
IT WAS LIKE THAT. I REMEMBERED I WAS THOR.
AND I REMEMBER THINKING THAT DONALD BLAKE WAS JUST A CHARACTER I'D BEEN PLAYING ALL THIS TIME.
BUT IT'S ALL GONE NOW AND I'M JUST ME AGAIN.
SO NOW THE SIXTY-FOUR THOUSAND DOLLAR QUESTION. WHAT ARE YOU GOING TO DO ABOUT IT?
DO? I HONESTLY DON'T KNOW. I THINK I NEED TO DO SOME EXPERIMENTATION WITH THE STICK, AND...
DON, PLEASE DON'T. PLEASE JUST...THROW THAT THING AWAY, OR GIVE IT TO SOME RESEARCHERS.
YOU DON'T KNOW WHAT YOU'RE DEALING WITH.

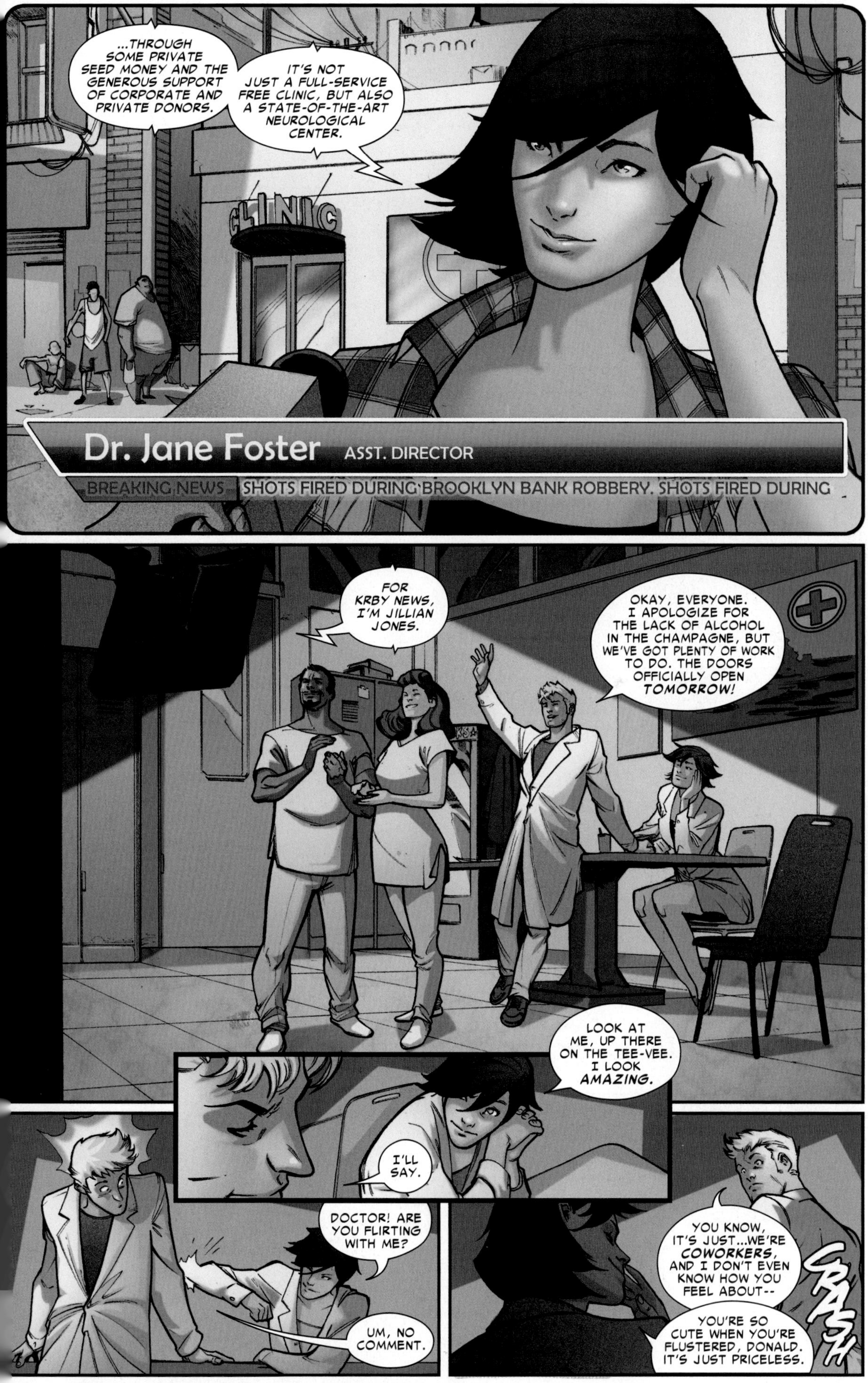
...THROUGH SOME PRIVATE SEED MONEY AND THE GENEROUS SUPPORT OF CORPORATE AND PRIVATE DONORS.
IT'S NOT JUST A FULL-SERVICE FREE CLINIC, BUT ALSO A STATE-OF-THE-ART NEUROLOGICAL CENTER.
CLINIC
Dr. Jane Foster ASST. DIRECTOR
BREAKING NEWS SHOTS FIRED DURING BROOKLYN BANK ROBBERY. SHOTS FIRED DURING
FOR KRBY NEWS, I'M JILLIAN JONES.
OKAY, EVERYONE. I APOLOGIZE FOR THE LACK OF ALCOHOL IN THE CHAMPAGNE, BUT WE'VE GOT PLENTY OF WORK TO DO. THE DOORS OFFICIALLY OPEN TOMORROW!
LOOK AT ME, UP THERE ON THE TEE-VEE. I LOOK AMAZING.
I'LL SAY.
DOCTOR! ARE YOU FLIRTING WITH ME?
UM, NO COMMENT.
YOU KNOW, IT'S JUST...WE'RE COWORKERS, AND I DON'T EVEN KNOW HOW YOU FEEL ABOUT--
YOU'RE SO CUTE WHEN YOU'RE FLUSTERED, DONALD. IT'S JUST PRICELESS.
CRASH

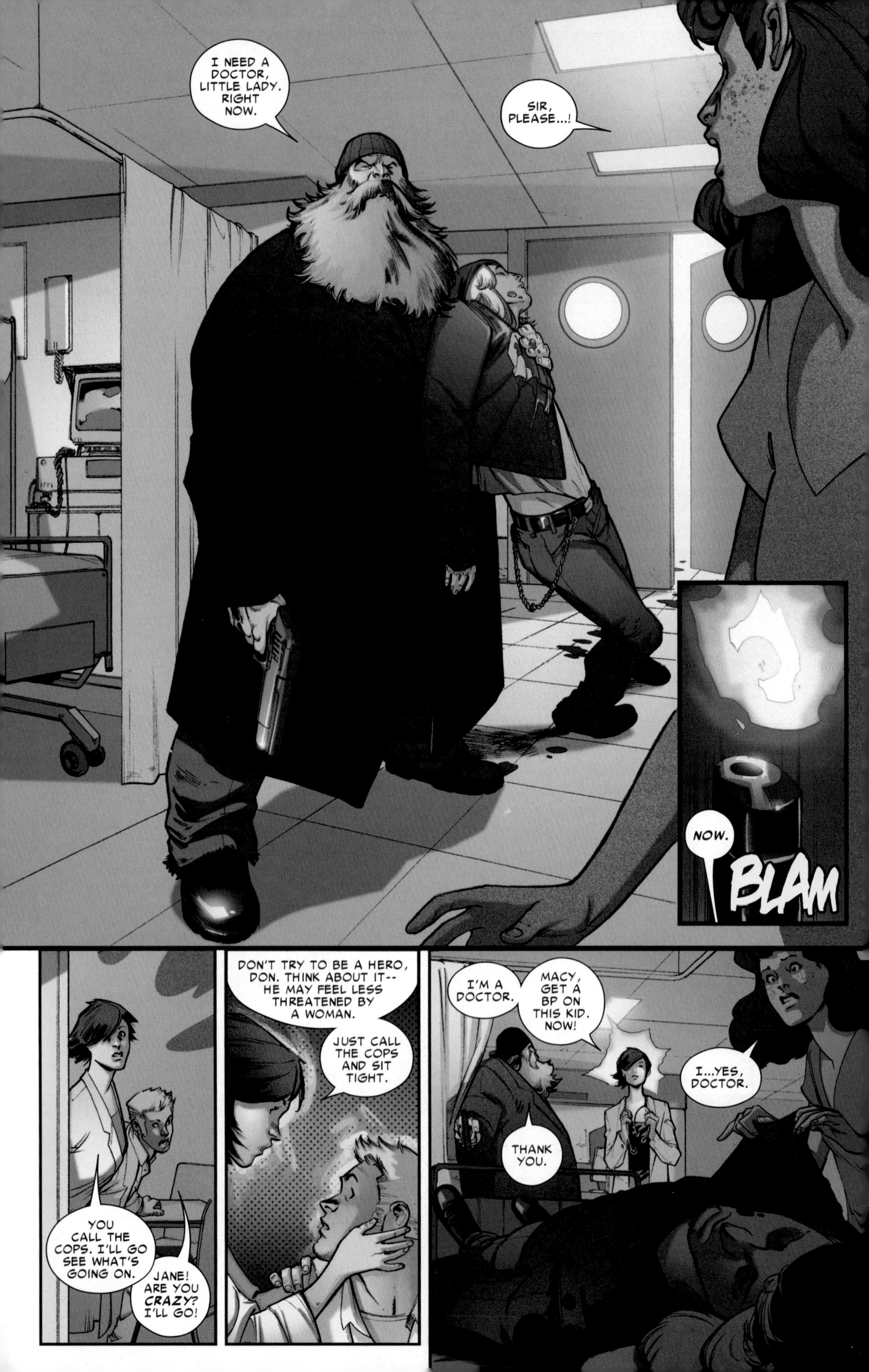
I NEED A DOCTOR, LITTLE LADY. RIGHT NOW.
SIR, PLEASE...!
NOW.
BLAM
YOU CALL THE COPS. I'LL GO SEE WHAT'S GOING ON.
JANE! ARE YOU *CRAZY*? I'LL GO!
DON'T TRY TO BE A HERO, DON. THINK ABOUT IT-- HE MAY FEEL LESS THREATENED BY A WOMAN.
JUST CALL THE COPS AND SIT TIGHT.
I'M A DOCTOR.
MACY, GET A BP ON THIS KID. NOW!
THANK YOU.
I...YES, DOCTOR.

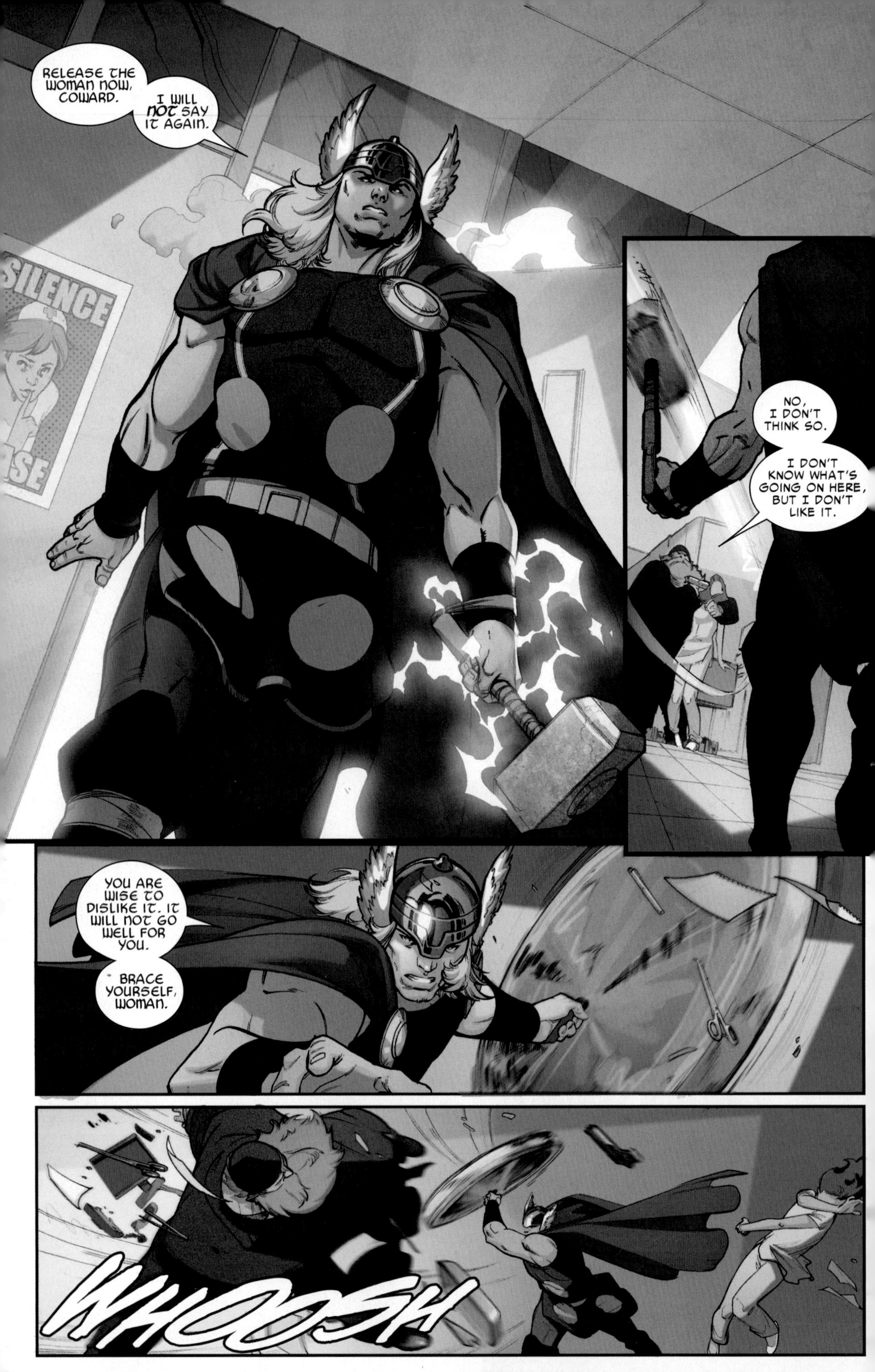

RELEASE THE WOMAN NOW, COWARD.
I WILL NOT SAY IT AGAIN.
SILENCE
NO, I DON'T THINK SO.
I DON'T KNOW WHAT'S GOING ON HERE, BUT I DON'T LIKE IT.
YOU ARE WISE TO DISLIKE IT. IT WILL NOT GO WELL FOR YOU.
BRACE YOURSELF, WOMAN.
WHOOSH

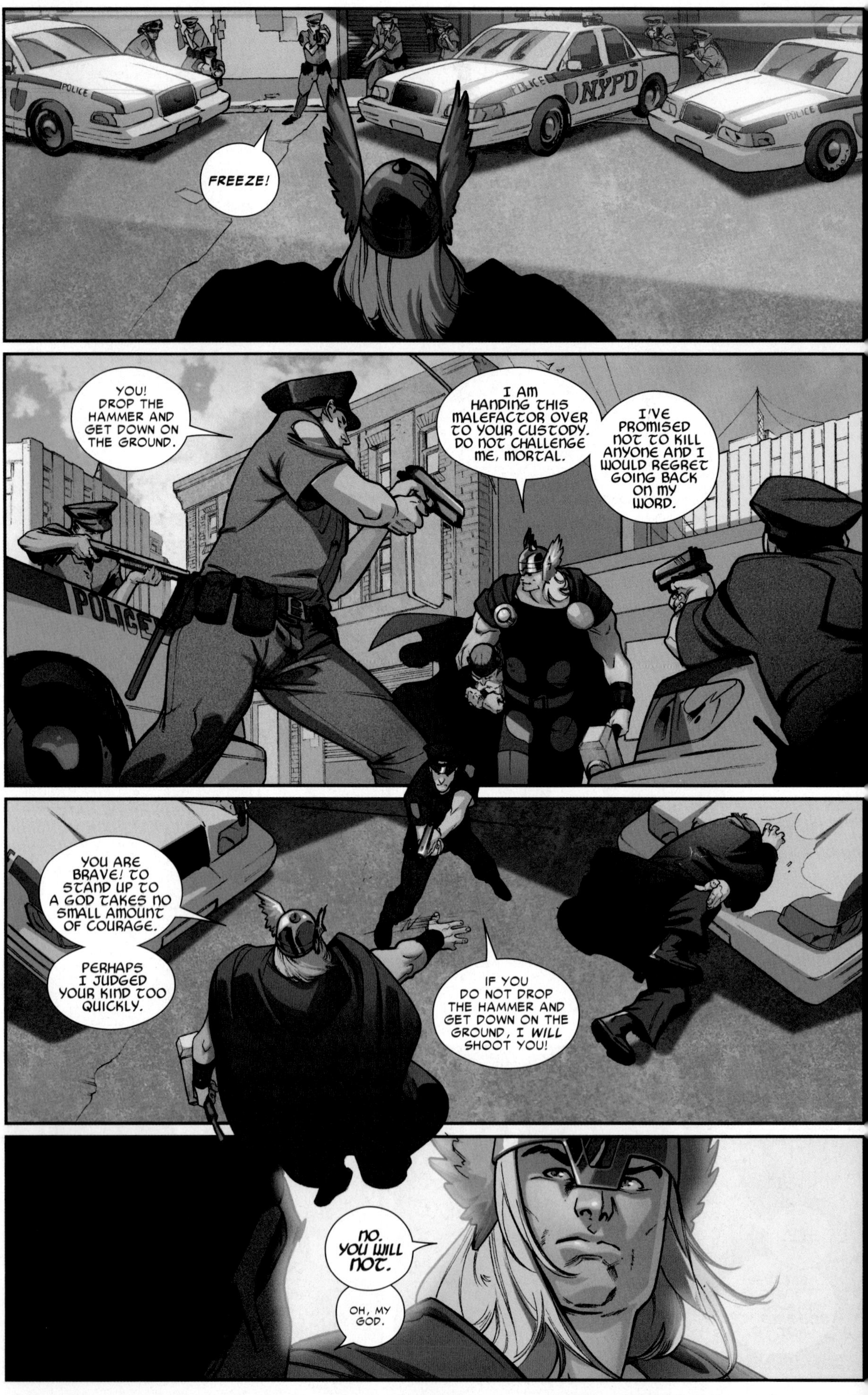
FREEZE!
YOU! DROP THE HAMMER AND GET DOWN ON THE GROUND.
I AM HANDING THIS MALEFACTOR OVER TO YOUR CUSTODY. DO NOT CHALLENGE ME, MORTAL.
I'VE PROMISED NOT TO KILL ANYONE AND I WOULD REGRET GOING BACK ON MY WORD.
YOU ARE BRAVE! TO STAND UP TO A GOD TAKES NO SMALL AMOUNT OF COURAGE.
PERHAPS I JUDGED YOUR KIND TOO QUICKLY.
IF YOU DO NOT DROP THE HAMMER AND GET DOWN ON THE GROUND, I WILL SHOOT YOU!
NO. YOU WILL NOT.
OH, MY GOD.

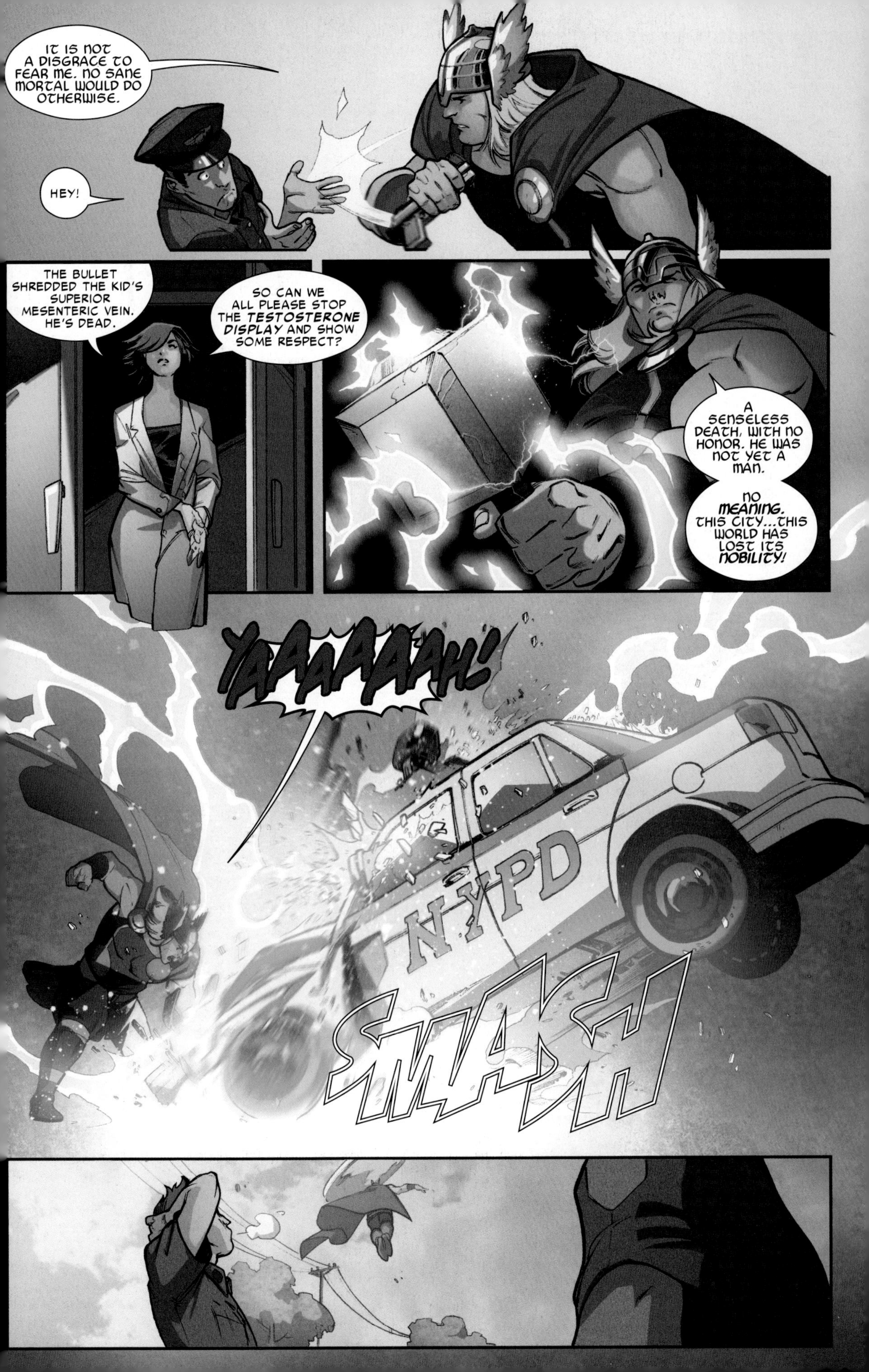
IT IS NOT A DISGRACE TO FEAR ME. NO SANE MORTAL WOULD DO OTHERWISE.
HEY!
THE BULLET SHREDDED THE KID'S SUPERIOR MESENTERIC VEIN. HE'S DEAD.
SO CAN WE ALL PLEASE STOP THE *TESTOSTERONE DISPLAY* AND SHOW SOME RESPECT?
A SENSELESS DEATH, WITH NO HONOR. HE WAS NOT YET A MAN.
NO ***MEANING.*** THIS CITY...THIS WORLD HAS LOST ITS ***NOBILITY!***
YAAAAAAH!
NYPD
SMASH

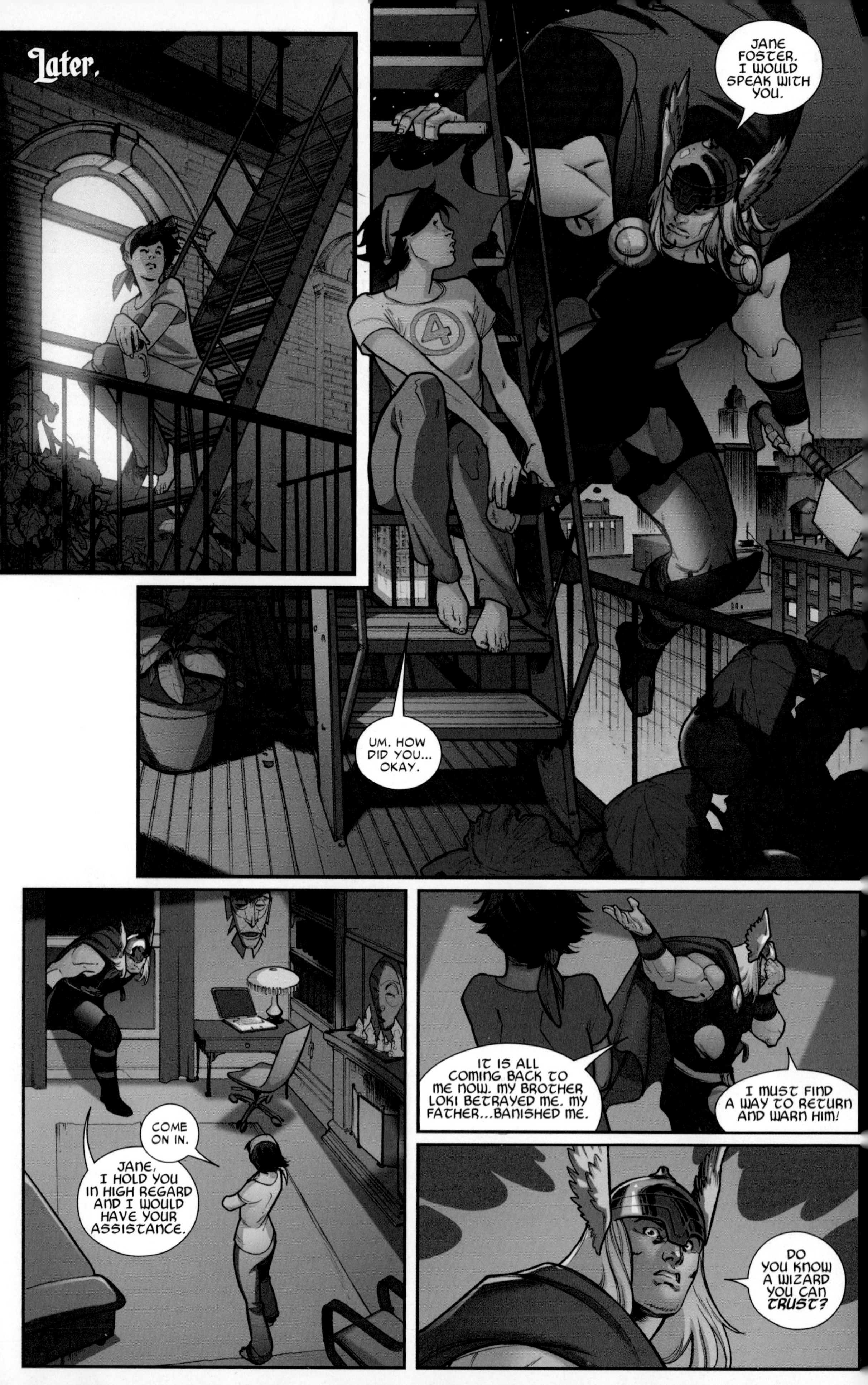
Later.
JANE FOSTER. I WOULD SPEAK WITH YOU.
UM. HOW DID YOU... OKAY.
COME ON IN.
JANE, I HOLD YOU IN HIGH REGARD AND I WOULD HAVE YOUR ASSISTANCE.
IT IS ALL COMING BACK TO ME NOW. MY BROTHER LOKI BETRAYED ME. MY FATHER...BANISHED ME.
I MUST FIND A WAY TO RETURN AND WARN HIM!
DO YOU KNOW A WIZARD YOU CAN TRUST?

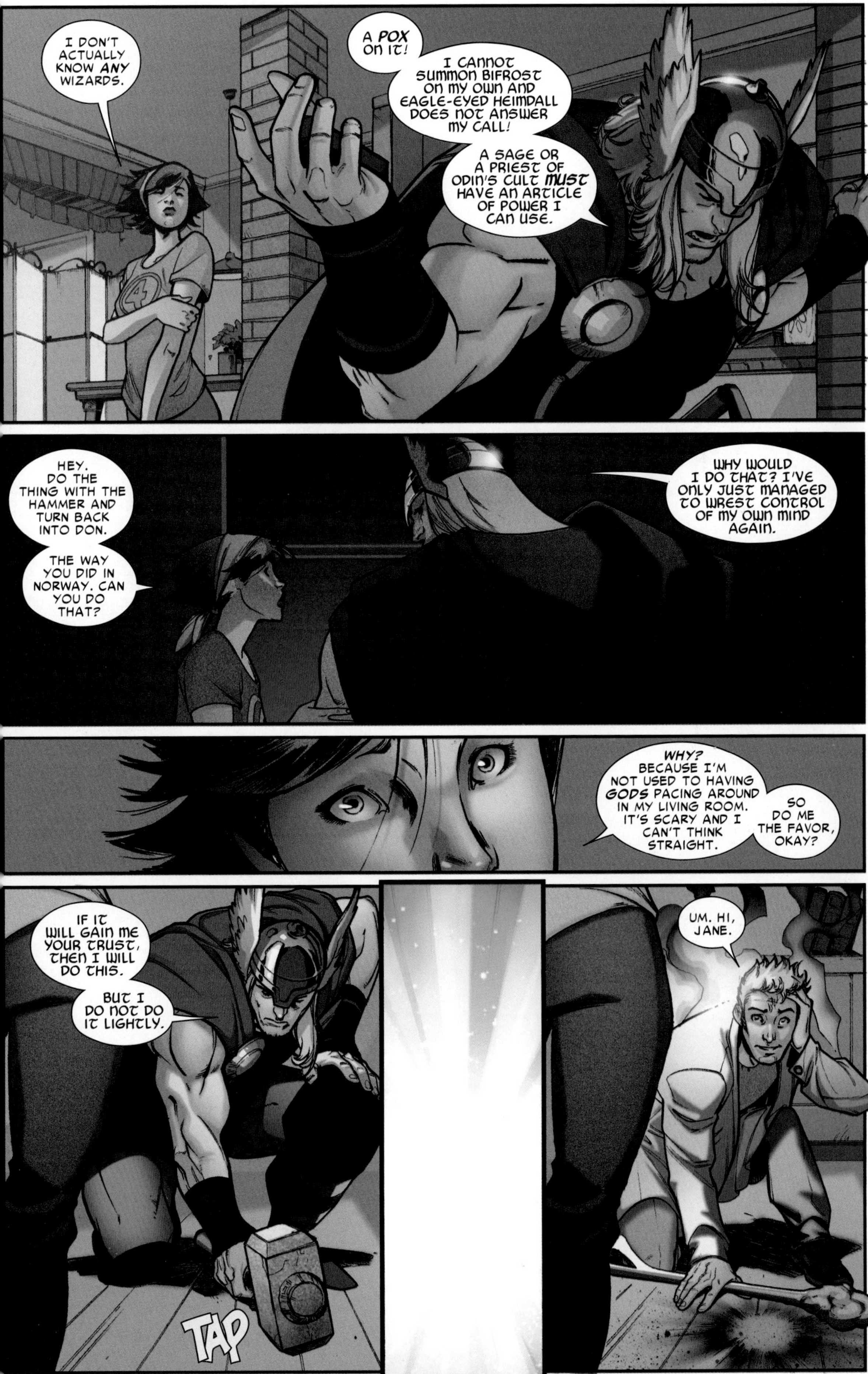
I DON'T ACTUALLY KNOW ANY WIZARDS.
A POX ON IT!
I CANNOT SUMMON BIFROST ON MY OWN AND EAGLE-EYED HEIMDALL DOES NOT ANSWER MY CALL!
A SAGE OR A PRIEST OF ODIN'S CULT MUST HAVE AN ARTICLE OF POWER I CAN USE.
HEY. DO THE THING WITH THE HAMMER AND TURN BACK INTO DON.
THE WAY YOU DID IN NORWAY. CAN YOU DO THAT?
WHY WOULD I DO THAT? I'VE ONLY JUST MANAGED TO WREST CONTROL OF MY OWN MIND AGAIN.
WHY? BECAUSE I'M NOT USED TO HAVING GODS PACING AROUND IN MY LIVING ROOM. IT'S SCARY AND I CAN'T THINK STRAIGHT.
SO DO ME THE FAVOR, OKAY?
IF IT WILL GAIN ME YOUR TRUST, THEN I WILL DO THIS.
BUT I DO NOT DO IT LIGHTLY.
TAP
UM. HI, JANE.

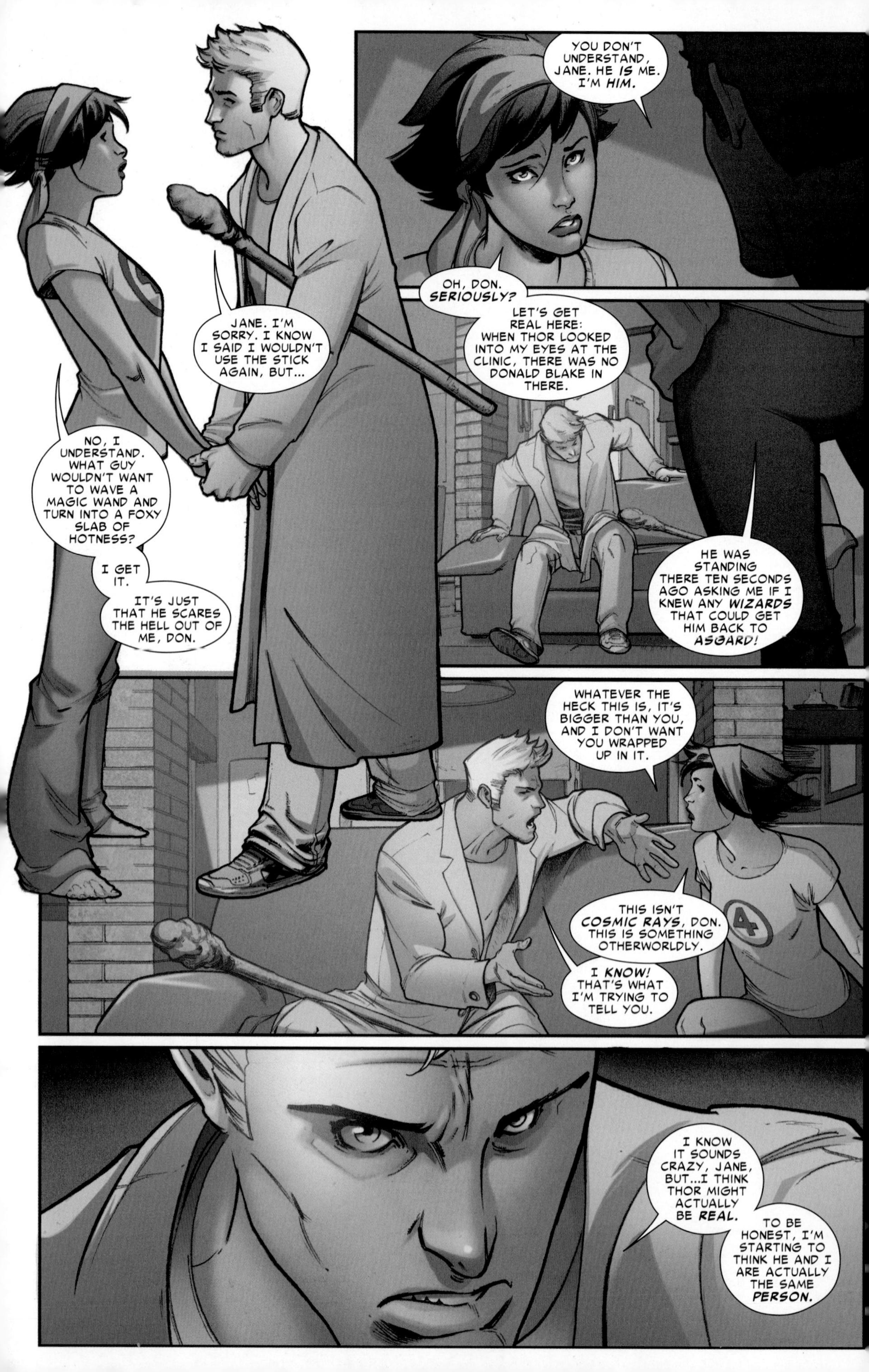
JANE. I'M SORRY. I KNOW I SAID I WOULDN'T USE THE STICK AGAIN, BUT...
NO, I UNDERSTAND. WHAT GUY WOULDN'T WANT TO WAVE A MAGIC WAND AND TURN INTO A FOXY SLAB OF HOTNESS?
I GET IT.
IT'S JUST THAT HE SCARES THE HELL OUT OF ME, DON.
YOU DON'T UNDERSTAND, JANE. HE *IS* ME. I'M *HIM*.
OH, DON. *SERIOUSLY?*
LET'S GET REAL HERE: WHEN THOR LOOKED INTO MY EYES AT THE CLINIC, THERE WAS NO DONALD BLAKE IN THERE.
HE WAS STANDING THERE TEN SECONDS AGO ASKING ME IF I KNEW ANY *WIZARDS* THAT COULD GET HIM BACK TO *ASGARD!*
WHATEVER THE HECK THIS IS, IT'S BIGGER THAN YOU, AND I DON'T WANT YOU WRAPPED UP IN IT.
THIS ISN'T *COSMIC RAYS*, DON. THIS IS SOMETHING OTHERWORLDLY.
I *KNOW!* THAT'S WHAT I'M TRYING TO TELL YOU.
I KNOW IT SOUNDS CRAZY, JANE, BUT...I THINK THOR MIGHT ACTUALLY BE *REAL*.
TO BE HONEST, I'M STARTING TO THINK HE AND I ARE ACTUALLY THE SAME *PERSON*.

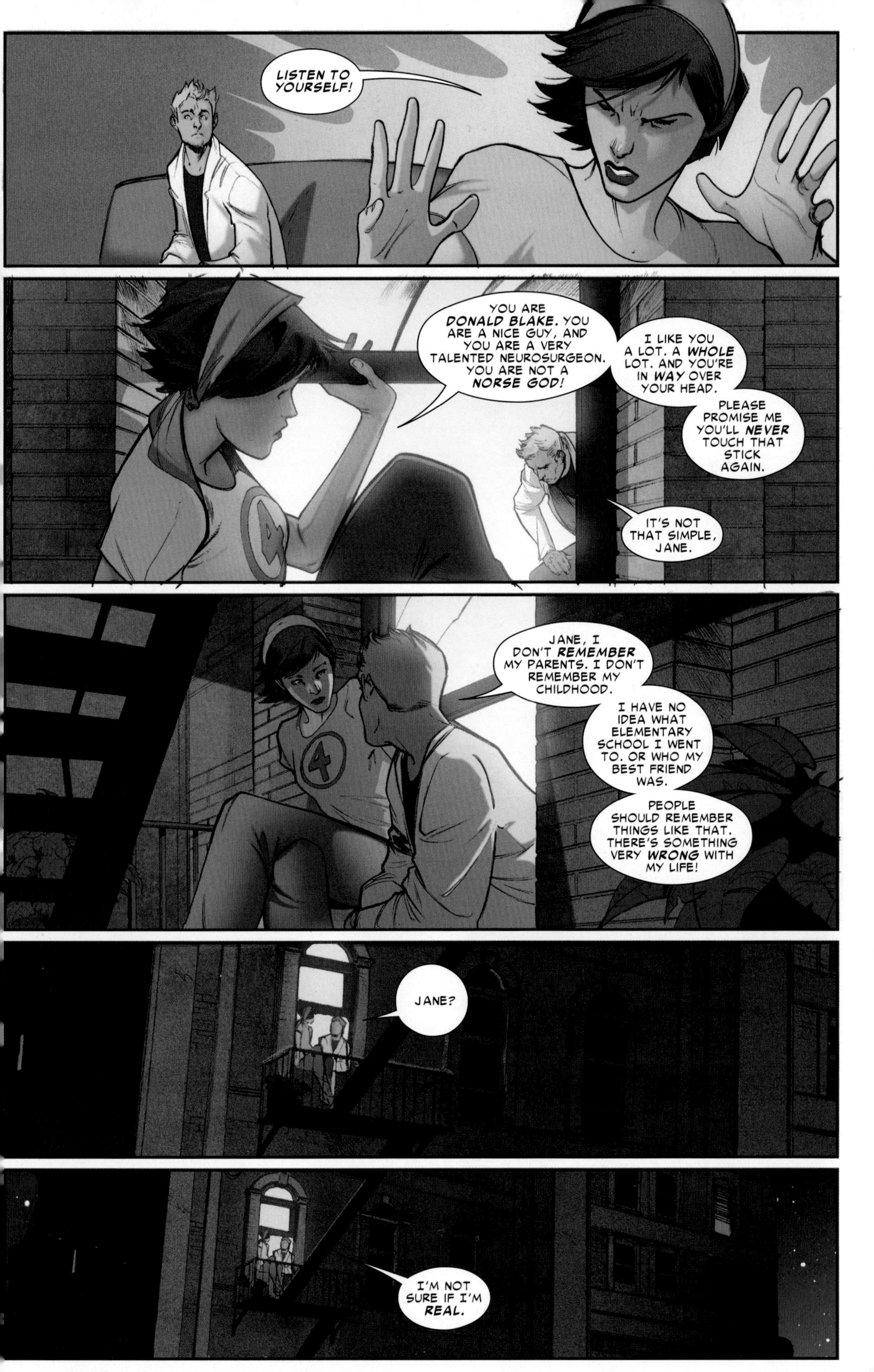
LISTEN TO YOURSELF!
YOU ARE DONALD BLAKE. YOU ARE A NICE GUY, AND YOU ARE A VERY TALENTED NEUROSURGEON. YOU ARE NOT A NORSE GOD!
I LIKE YOU A LOT. A WHOLE LOT. AND YOU'RE IN WAY OVER YOUR HEAD.
PLEASE PROMISE ME YOU'LL NEVER TOUCH THAT STICK AGAIN.
IT'S NOT THAT SIMPLE, JANE.
JANE, I DON'T REMEMBER MY PARENTS. I DON'T REMEMBER MY CHILDHOOD.
I HAVE NO IDEA WHAT ELEMENTARY SCHOOL I WENT TO. OR WHO MY BEST FRIEND WAS.
PEOPLE SHOULD REMEMBER THINGS LIKE THAT. THERE'S SOMETHING VERY WRONG WITH MY LIFE!
JANE?
I'M NOT SURE IF I'M REAL.

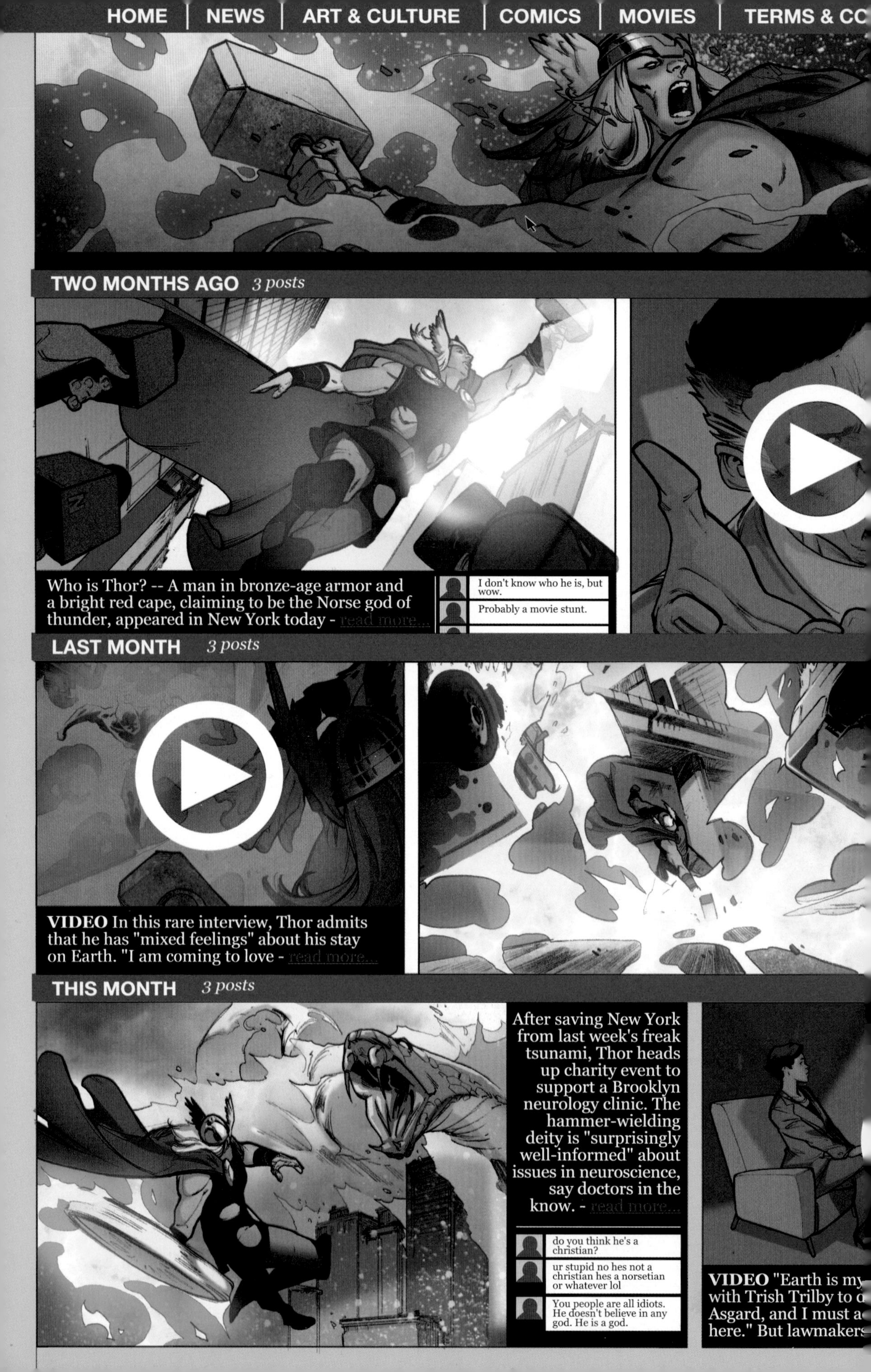
HOME | NEWS | ART & CULTURE | COMICS | MOVIES | TERMS & CO
TWO MONTHS AGO 3 posts
Who is Thor? -- A man in bronze-age armor and a bright red cape, claiming to be the Norse god of thunder, appeared in New York today - read more...
I don't know who he is, but wow.
Probably a movie stunt.
LAST MONTH 3 posts
VIDEO In this rare interview, Thor admits that he has "mixed feelings" about his stay on Earth. "I am coming to love - read more...
THIS MONTH 3 posts
After saving New York from last week's freak tsunami, Thor heads up charity event to support a Brooklyn neurology clinic. The hammer-wielding deity is "surprisingly well-informed" about issues in neuroscience, say doctors in the know. - read more...
do you think he's a christian?
ur stupid no hes not a christian hes a norsetian or whatever lol
You people are all idiots. He doesn't believe in any god. He is a god.
VIDEO "Earth is my
with Trish Trilby to
Asgard, and I must a
here." But lawmakers

WE ADORE THOR!
News & notes on everyone's fave norse god!

VIDEO Daily Bugle Editor J. Jonah Jameson on Thor. "I like a man who isn't afraid to show his face to the world."

FIRST!!!! O_o

People still read newspapers?

Nice 'stache. Welcome to the 19th century, dude!

Thor shows off his "heavenly" abs while fighting "Carbon Copy Man." - many more pix

❤❤❤ YUMMY ❤❤❤

I want to go to there. XD

You ladies realize you

Twitter explodes as Thor beats up a parking lot in midtown, screaming "Father! Father! Hear me!" over and over again. - read more...

SMASH UP ALL THE THINGS!

oh, he looks so sad. would love 2 give him a hug <3

Which blond hunk is in talks to play Thor in new biopic? "I'll have to get in much better shape," he jokes. - click to reveal his identity

w." A hopeful Thor sits down s future. "I have been exiled from he says. "I can do much good ce don't necessarily - read more...

Thor has never used the Internet! "They tell me it is a great box filled with kittens. I do not understand the need for it."

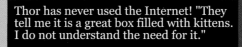

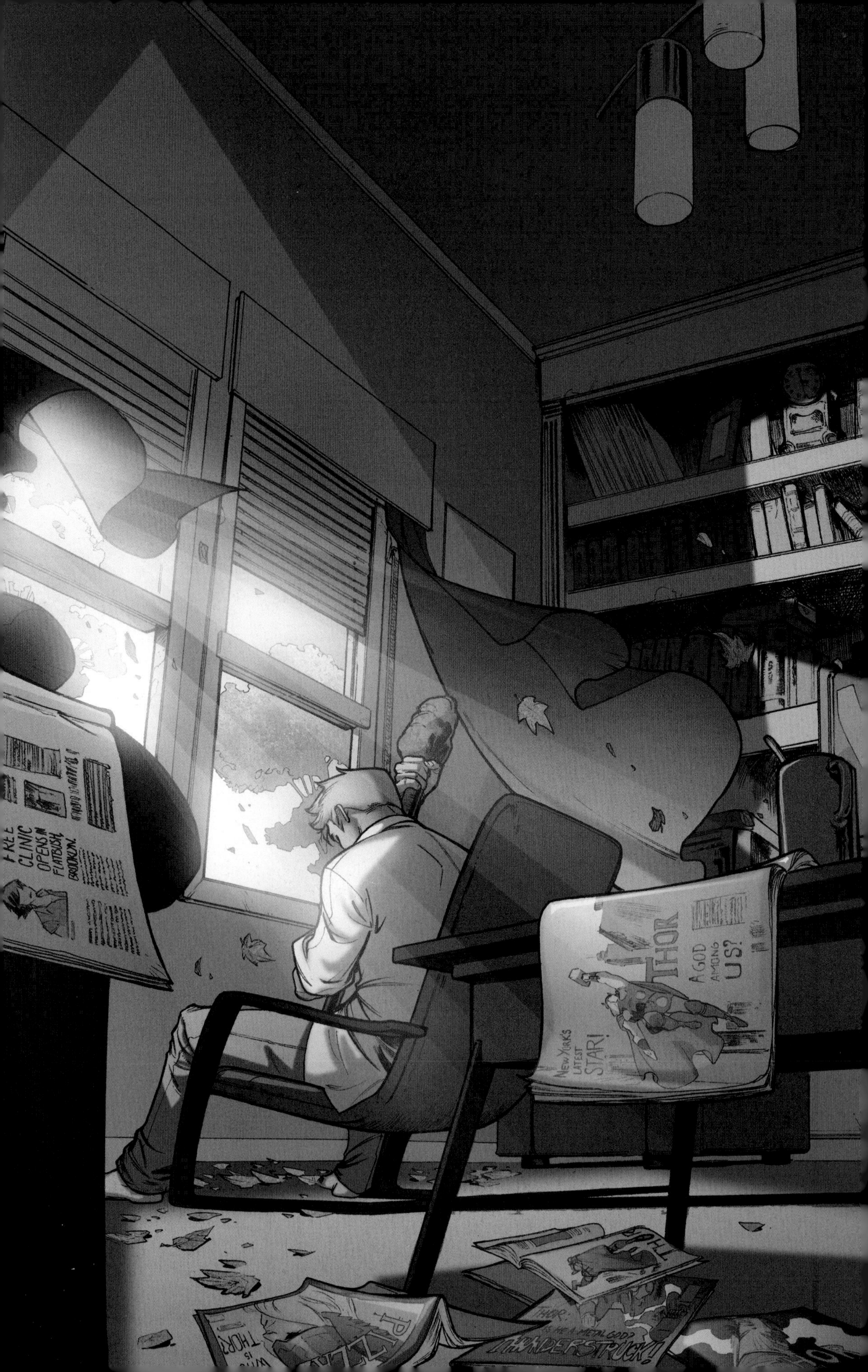

FREE CLINIC OPENS IN FLATBUSH, BROOKLYN.
THOR
A GOD AMONG US?
NEW YORK'S LATEST STAR!
WHO IS THOR?
THOR:
IS HE A METAL GOD?
THUNDERSTRUCK!

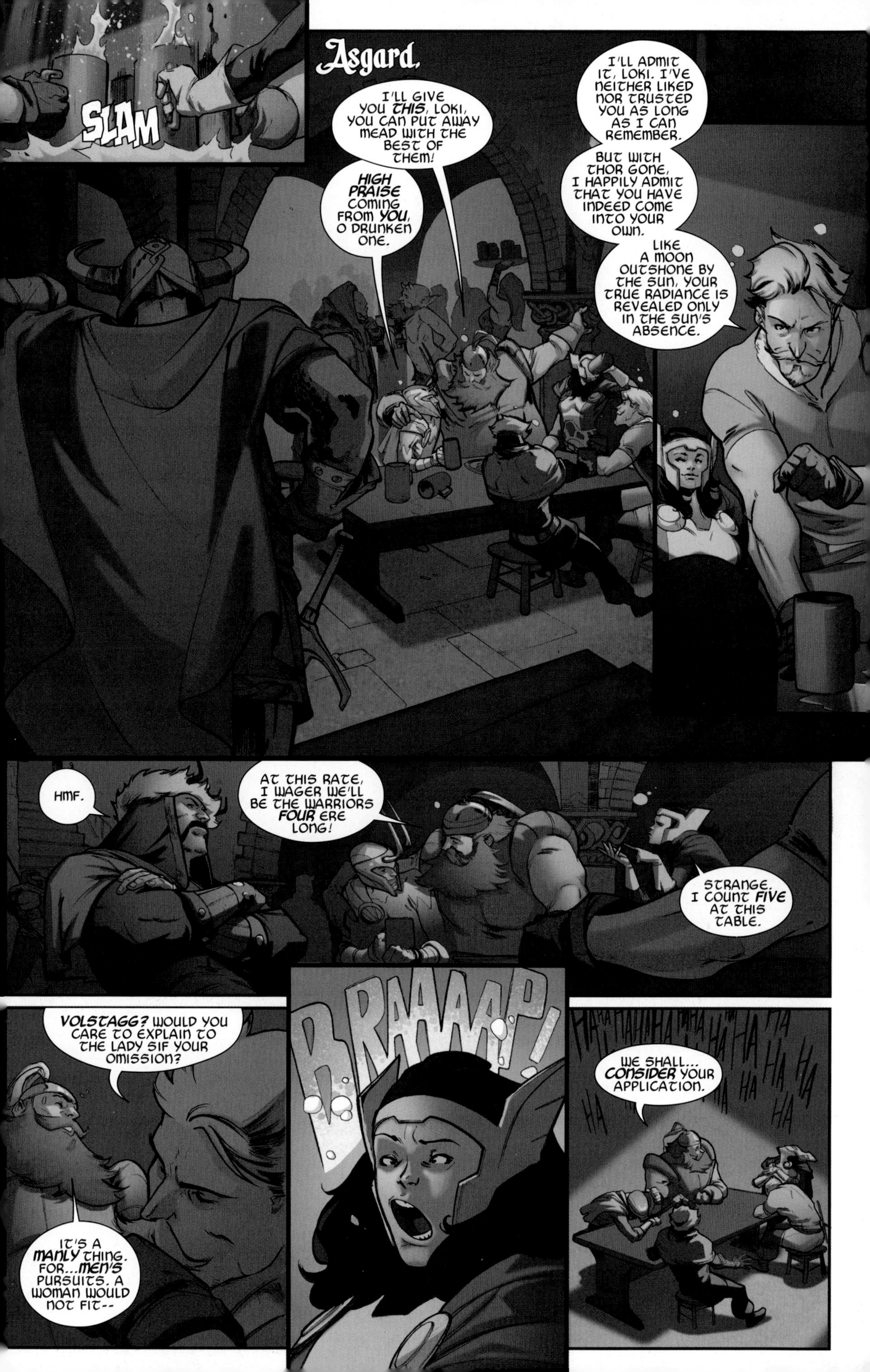
SLAM
Asgard.
I'LL GIVE YOU THIS, LOKI, YOU CAN PUT AWAY MEAD WITH THE BEST OF THEM!
HIGH PRAISE COMING FROM YOU, O DRUNKEN ONE.
I'LL ADMIT IT, LOKI. I'VE NEITHER LIKED NOR TRUSTED YOU AS LONG AS I CAN REMEMBER.
BUT WITH THOR GONE, I HAPPILY ADMIT THAT YOU HAVE INDEED COME INTO YOUR OWN.
LIKE A MOON OUTSHONE BY THE SUN, YOUR TRUE RADIANCE IS REVEALED ONLY IN THE SUN'S ABSENCE.
HMF.
AT THIS RATE, I WAGER WE'LL BE THE WARRIORS FOUR ERE LONG!
STRANGE. I COUNT FIVE AT THIS TABLE.
VOLSTAGG? WOULD YOU CARE TO EXPLAIN TO THE LADY SIF YOUR OMISSION?
IT'S A MANLY THING. FOR...MEN'S PURSUITS. A WOMAN WOULD NOT FIT--
BRAAAAP!
WE SHALL... CONSIDER YOUR APPLICATION.

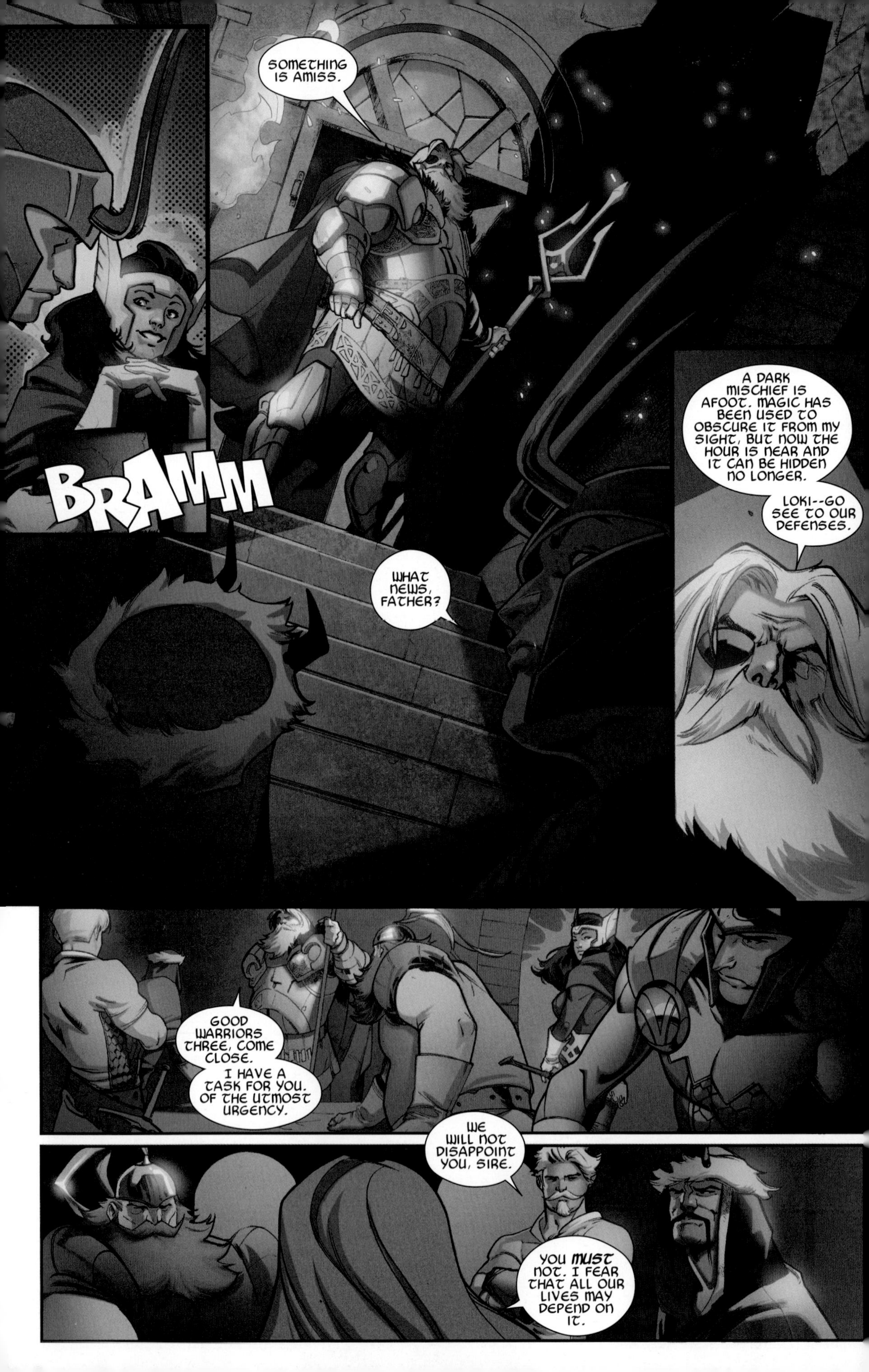
SOMETHING IS AMISS.
BRAMM
WHAT NEWS, FATHER?
A DARK MISCHIEF IS AFOOT. MAGIC HAS BEEN USED TO OBSCURE IT FROM MY SIGHT, BUT NOW THE HOUR IS NEAR AND IT CAN BE HIDDEN NO LONGER.
LOKI--GO SEE TO OUR DEFENSES.
GOOD WARRIORS THREE, COME CLOSE.
I HAVE A TASK FOR YOU. OF THE UTMOST URGENCY.
WE WILL NOT DISAPPOINT YOU, SIRE.
YOU MUST NOT. I FEAR THAT ALL OUR LIVES MAY DEPEND ON IT.

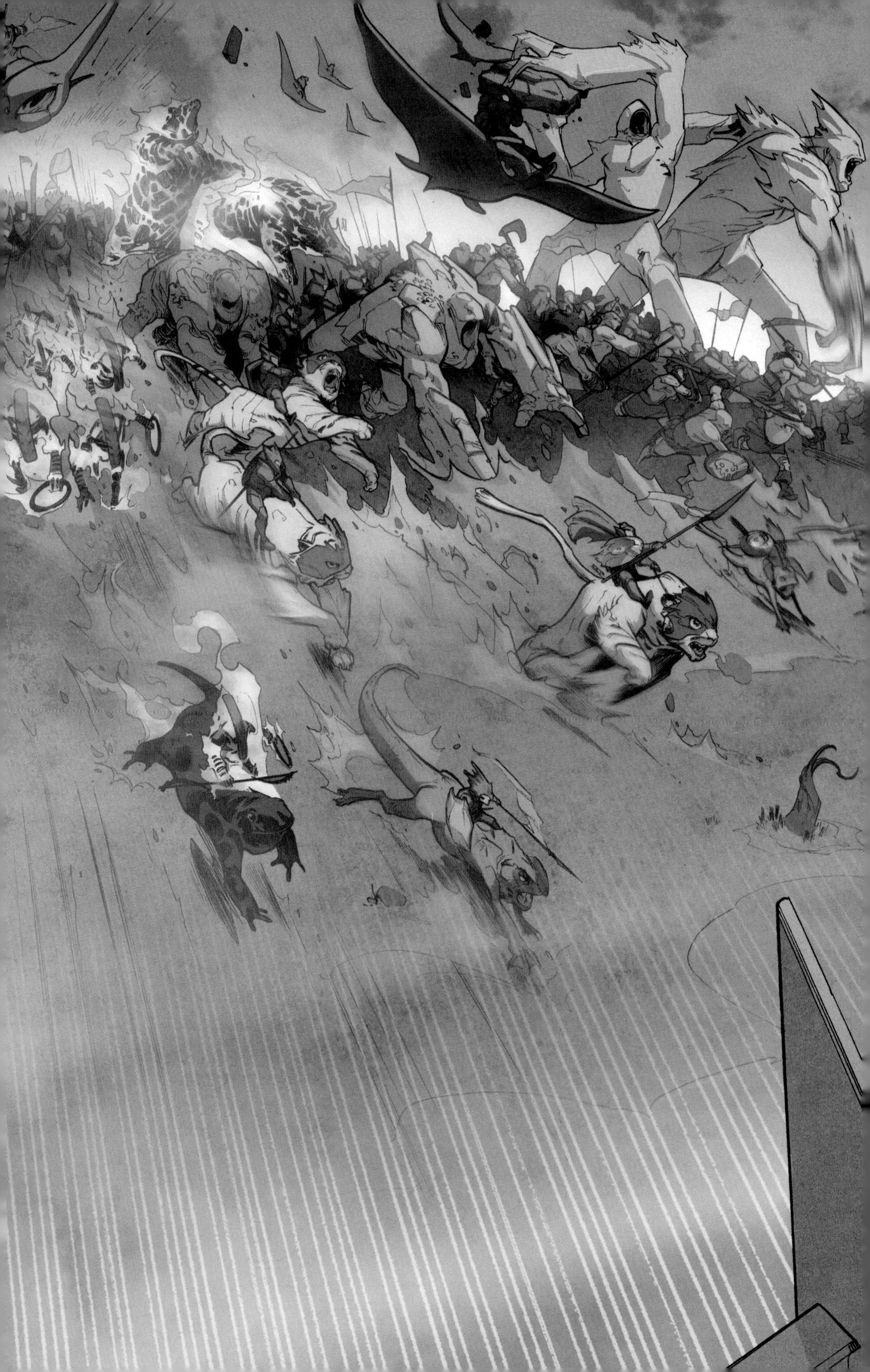

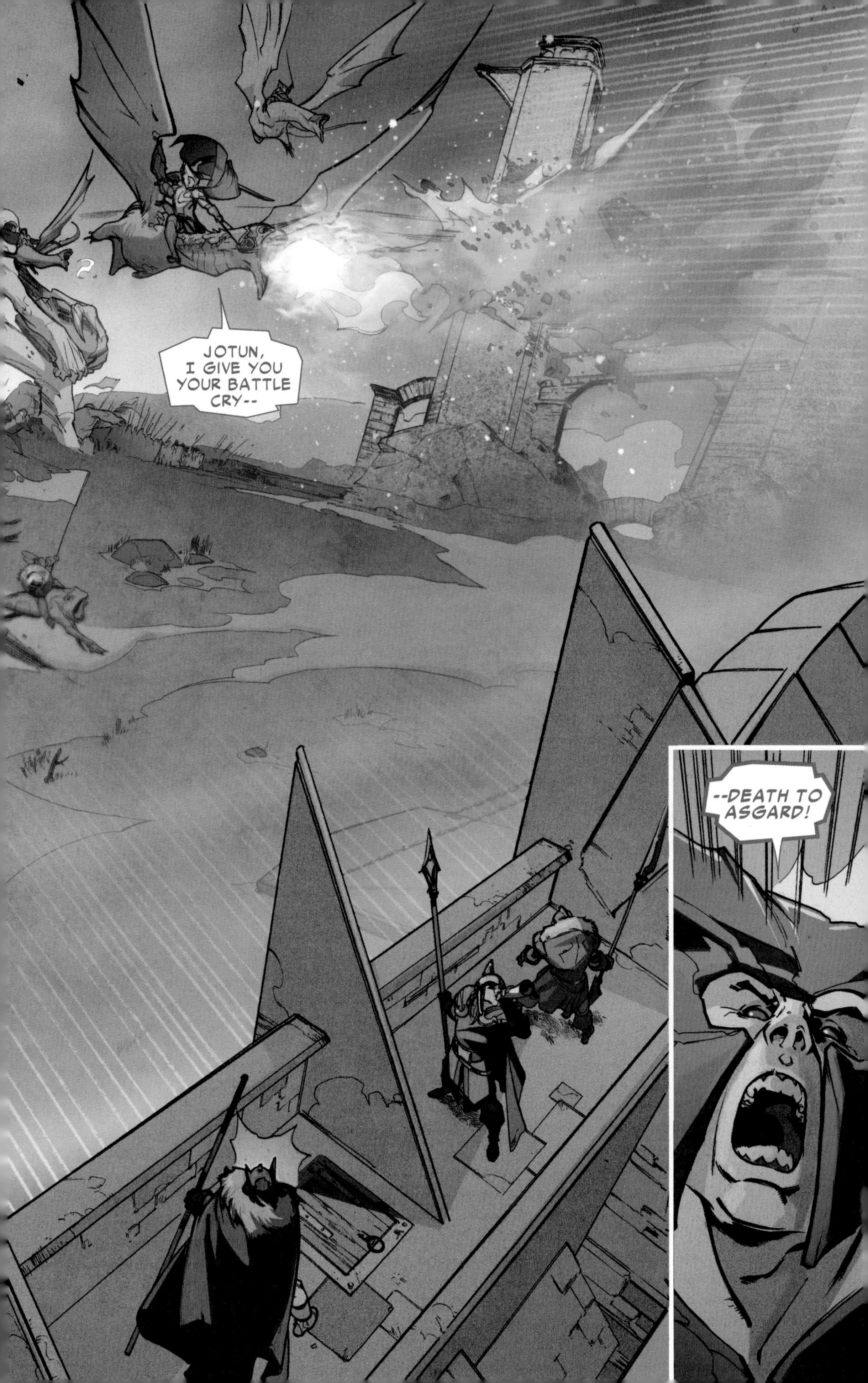
JOTUN, I GIVE YOU YOUR BATTLE CRY--
--DEATH TO ASGARD!

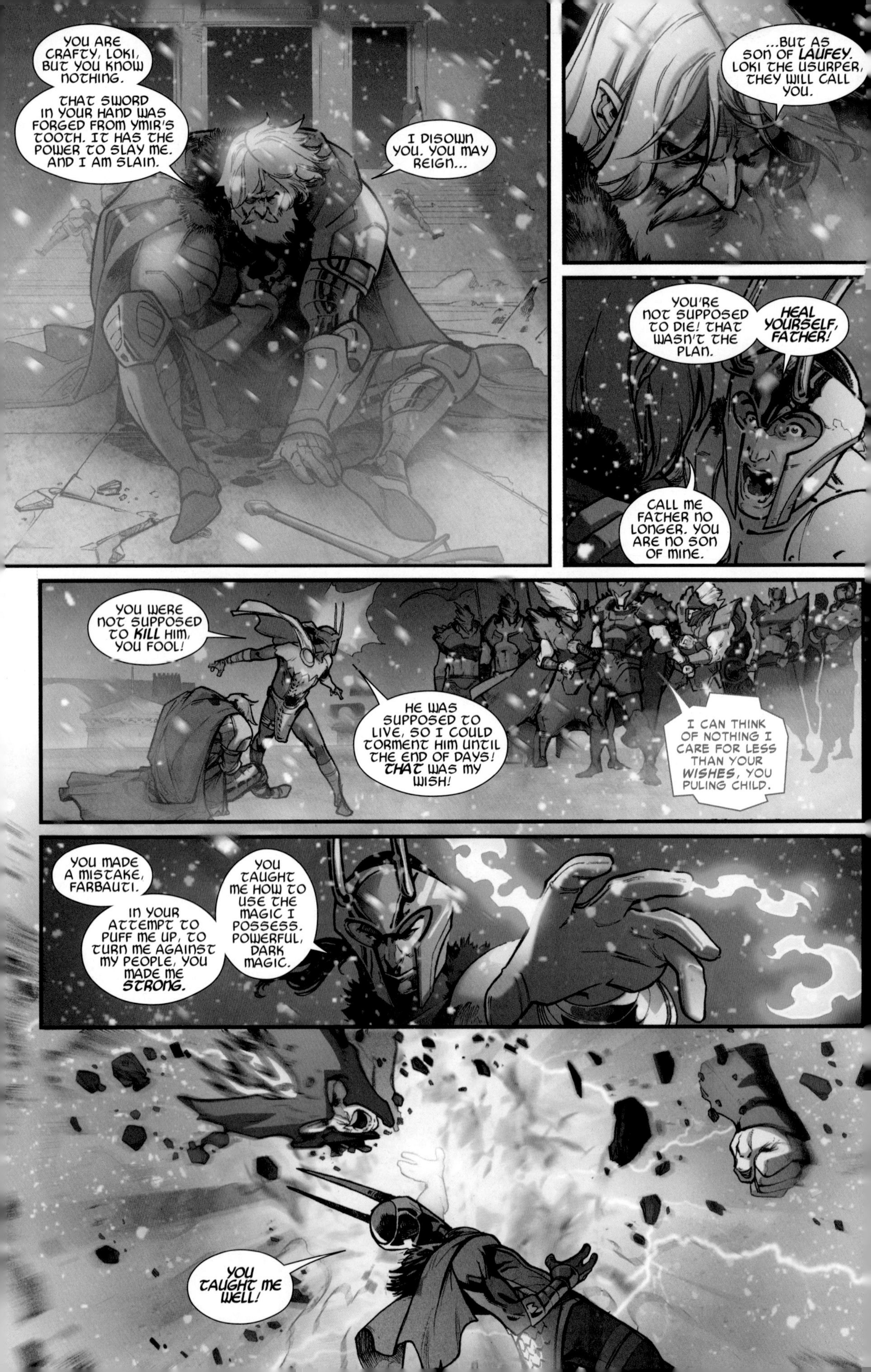
YOU ARE CRAFTY, LOKI, BUT YOU KNOW NOTHING.
THAT SWORD IN YOUR HAND WAS FORGED FROM YMIR'S TOOTH. IT HAS THE POWER TO SLAY ME. AND I AM SLAIN.
I DISOWN YOU. YOU MAY REIGN...
...BUT AS SON OF LAUFEY. LOKI THE USURPER, THEY WILL CALL YOU.
YOU'RE NOT SUPPOSED TO DIE! THAT WASN'T THE PLAN.
HEAL YOURSELF, FATHER!
CALL ME FATHER NO LONGER. YOU ARE NO SON OF MINE.
YOU WERE NOT SUPPOSED TO KILL HIM, YOU FOOL!
HE WAS SUPPOSED TO LIVE, SO I COULD TORMENT HIM UNTIL THE END OF DAYS! THAT WAS MY WISH!
I CAN THINK OF NOTHING I CARE FOR LESS THAN YOUR WISHES, YOU PULING CHILD.
YOU MADE A MISTAKE, FARBAUTI.
IN YOUR ATTEMPT TO PUFF ME UP, TO TURN ME AGAINST MY PEOPLE, YOU MADE ME STRONG.
YOU TAUGHT ME HOW TO USE THE MAGIC I POSSESS. POWERFUL, DARK MAGIC.
YOU TAUGHT ME WELL!

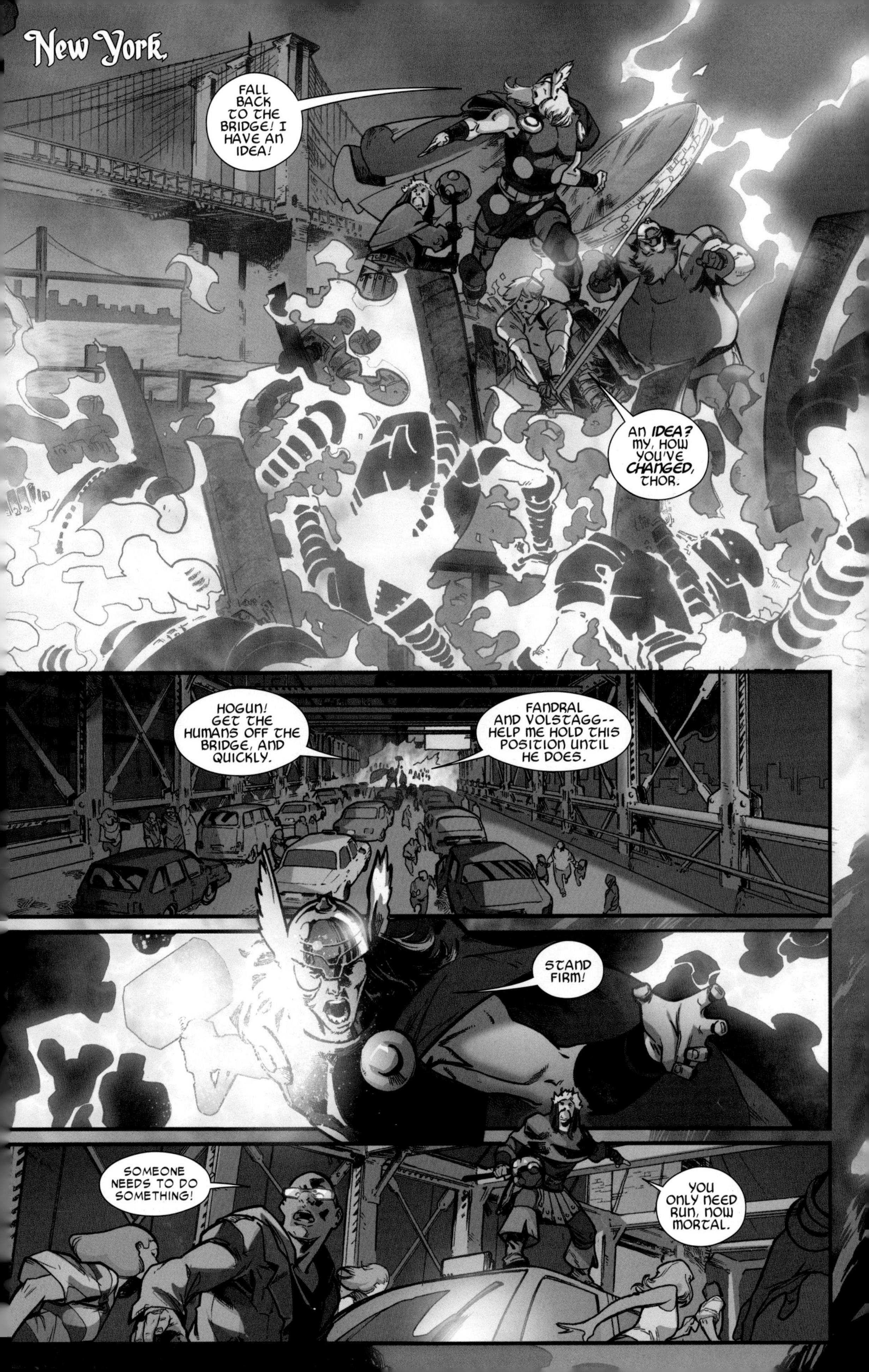
New York.
FALL BACK TO THE BRIDGE! I HAVE AN IDEA!
AN IDEA? MY, HOW YOU'VE CHANGED, THOR.
HOGUN! GET THE HUMANS OFF THE BRIDGE, AND QUICKLY.
FANDRAL AND VOLSTAGG-- HELP ME HOLD THIS POSITION UNTIL HE DOES.
STAND FIRM!
SOMEONE NEEDS TO DO SOMETHING!
YOU ONLY NEED RUN, NOW MORTAL.

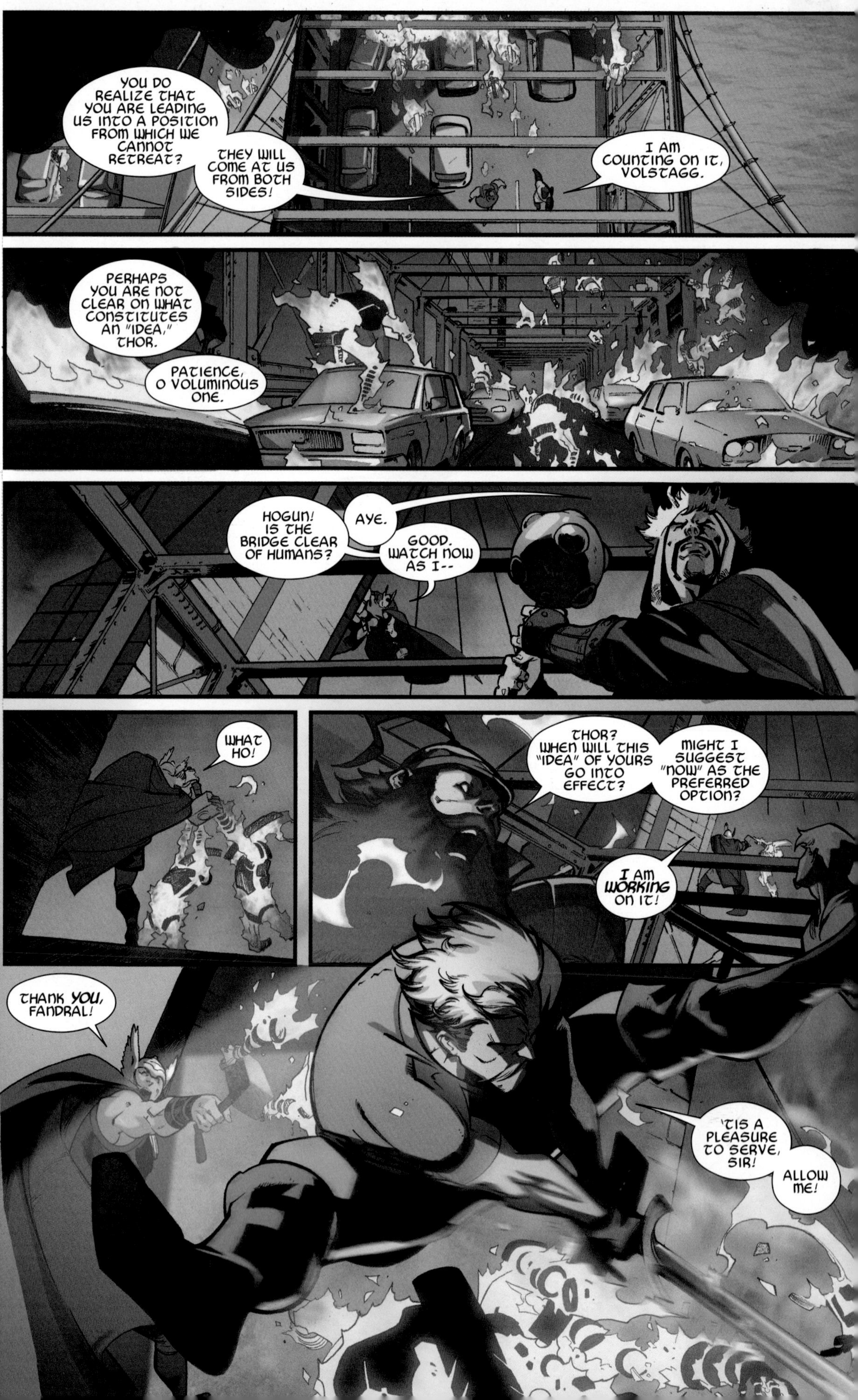
YOU DO REALIZE THAT YOU ARE LEADING US INTO A POSITION FROM WHICH WE CANNOT RETREAT?
THEY WILL COME AT US FROM BOTH SIDES!
I AM COUNTING ON IT, VOLSTAGG.
PERHAPS YOU ARE NOT CLEAR ON WHAT CONSTITUTES AN "IDEA," THOR.
PATIENCE, O VOLUMINOUS ONE.
HOGUN! IS THE BRIDGE CLEAR OF HUMANS?
AYE.
GOOD. WATCH NOW AS I--
WHAT HO!
THOR? WHEN WILL THIS "IDEA" OF YOURS GO INTO EFFECT?
MIGHT I SUGGEST "NOW" AS THE PREFERRED OPTION?
I AM WORKING ON IT!
THANK YOU, FANDRAL!
'TIS A PLEASURE TO SERVE, SIR!
ALLOW ME!

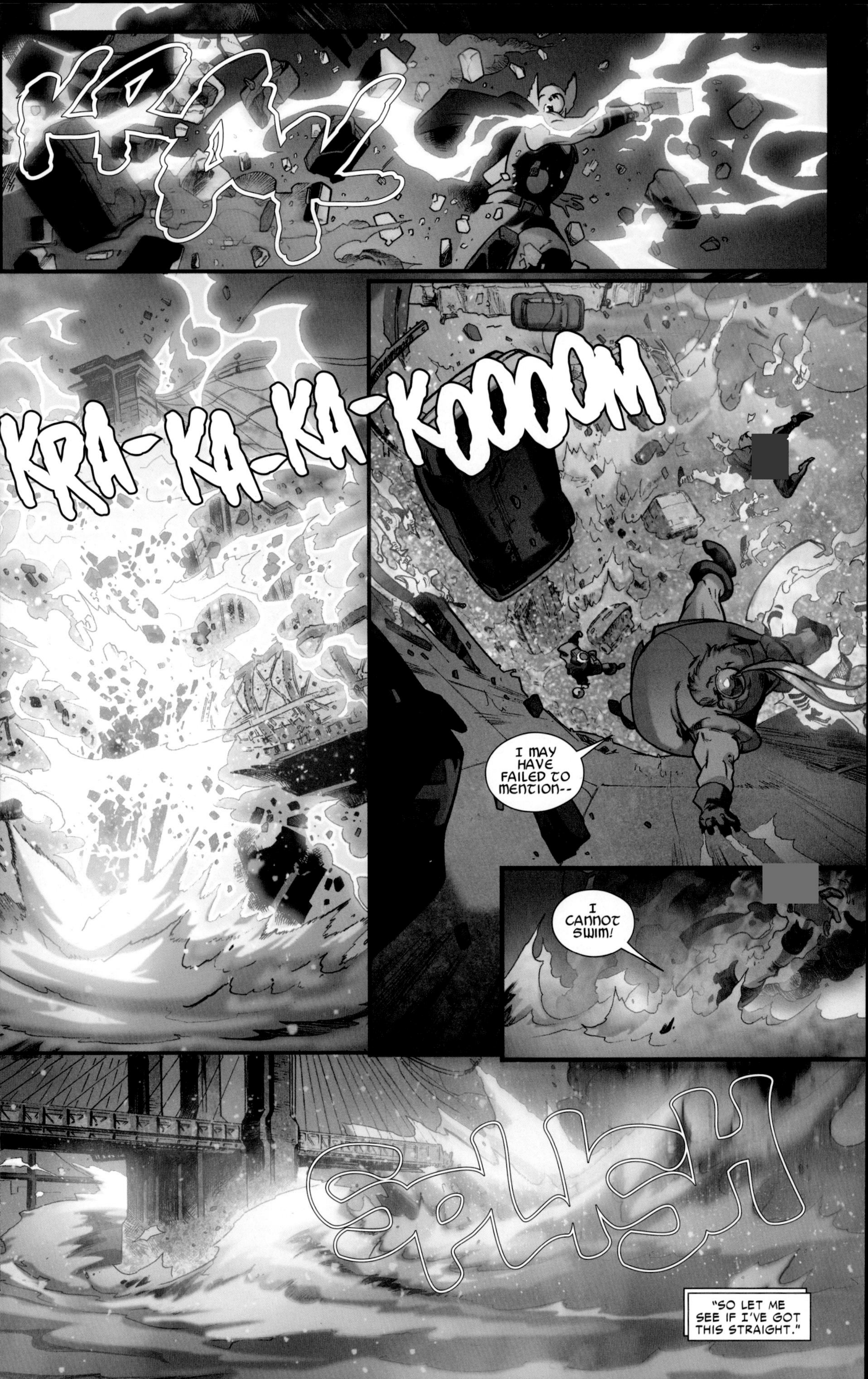
KRA-KA-KA-KOOOOM
I MAY HAVE FAILED TO MENTION--
I CANNOT SWIM!
"SO LET ME SEE IF I'VE GOT THIS STRAIGHT."

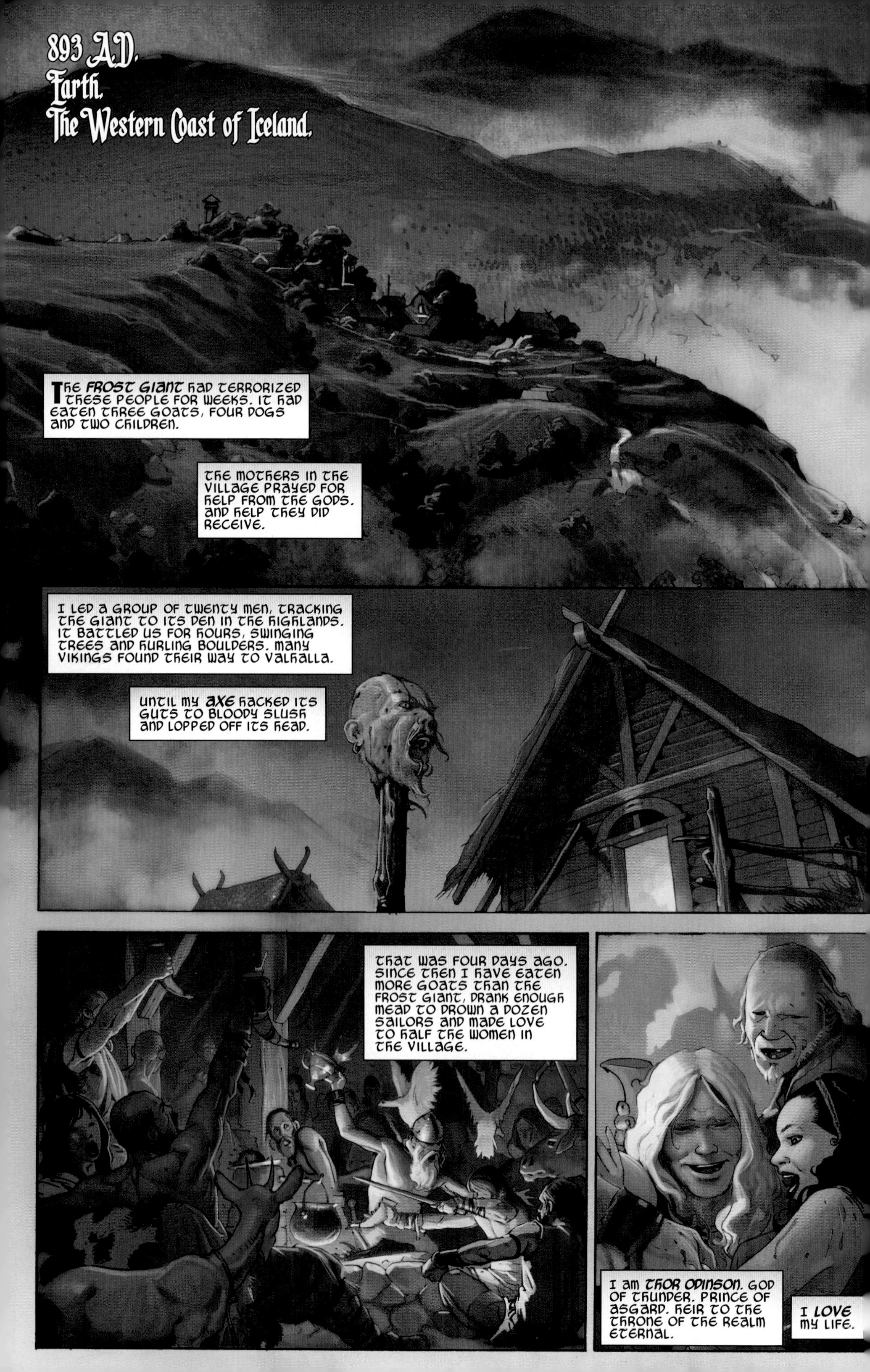
893 A.D.
Earth.
The Western Coast of Iceland.
THE FROST GIANT HAD TERRORIZED THESE PEOPLE FOR WEEKS. IT HAD EATEN THREE GOATS, FOUR DOGS AND TWO CHILDREN.
THE MOTHERS IN THE VILLAGE PRAYED FOR HELP FROM THE GODS. AND HELP THEY DID RECEIVE.
I LED A GROUP OF TWENTY MEN, TRACKING THE GIANT TO ITS DEN IN THE HIGHLANDS. IT BATTLED US FOR HOURS, SWINGING TREES AND HURLING BOULDERS. MANY VIKINGS FOUND THEIR WAY TO VALHALLA.
UNTIL MY AXE HACKED ITS GUTS TO BLOODY SLUSH AND LOPPED OFF ITS HEAD.
THAT WAS FOUR DAYS AGO. SINCE THEN I HAVE EATEN MORE GOATS THAN THE FROST GIANT, DRANK ENOUGH MEAD TO DROWN A DOZEN SAILORS AND MADE LOVE TO HALF THE WOMEN IN THE VILLAGE.
I AM THOR ODINSON. GOD OF THUNDER. PRINCE OF ASGARD. HEIR TO THE THRONE OF THE REALM ETERNAL.
I LOVE MY LIFE.

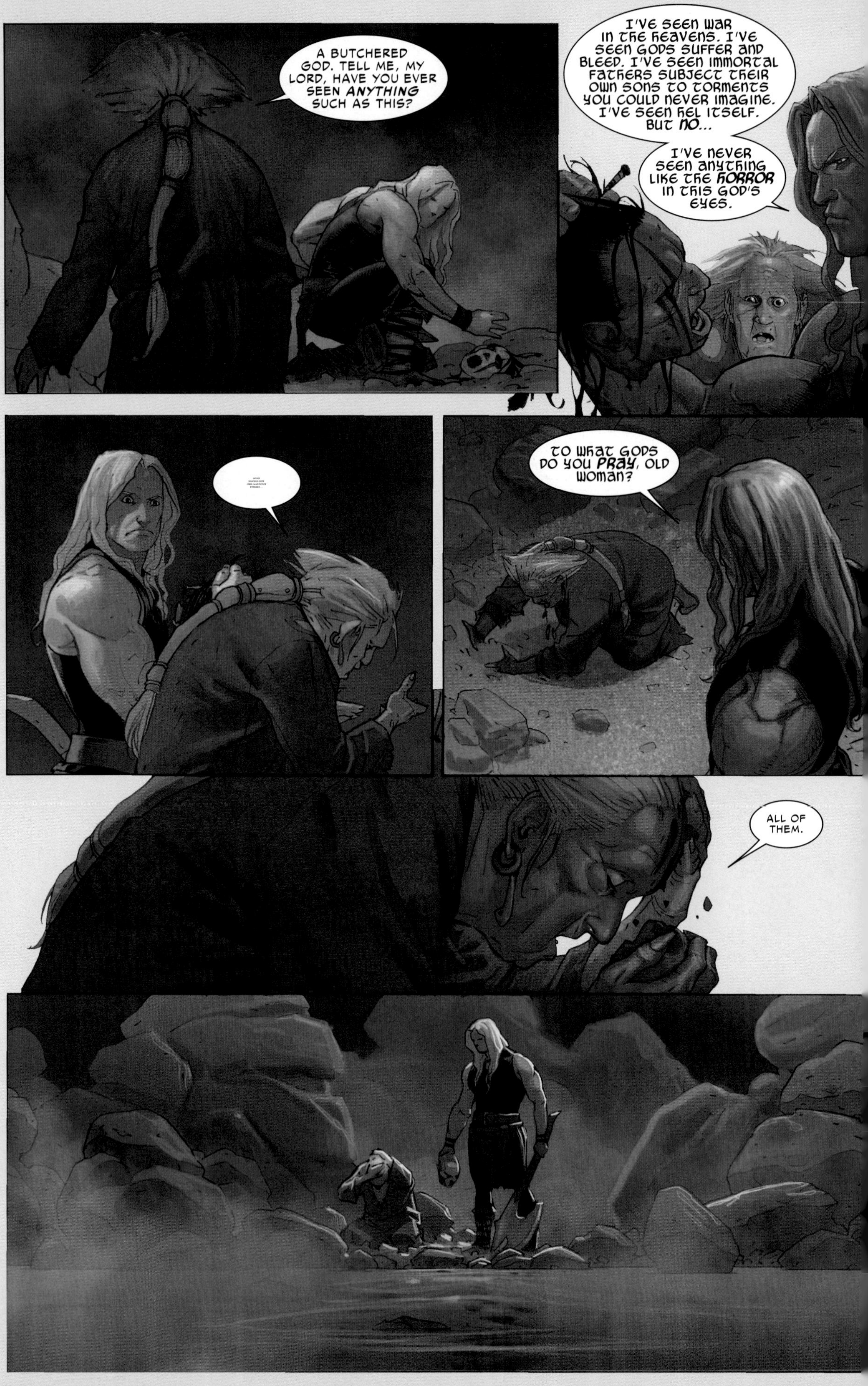
A BUTCHERED GOD. TELL ME, MY LORD, HAVE YOU EVER SEEN ANYTHING SUCH AS THIS?
I'VE SEEN WAR IN THE HEAVENS. I'VE SEEN GODS SUFFER AND BLEED. I'VE SEEN IMMORTAL FATHERS SUBJECT THEIR OWN SONS TO TORMENTS YOU COULD NEVER IMAGINE. I'VE SEEN HEL ITSELF. BUT NO...
I'VE NEVER SEEN ANYTHING LIKE THE HORROR IN THIS GOD'S EYES.
TO WHAT GODS DO YOU PRAY, OLD WOMAN?
ALL OF THEM.

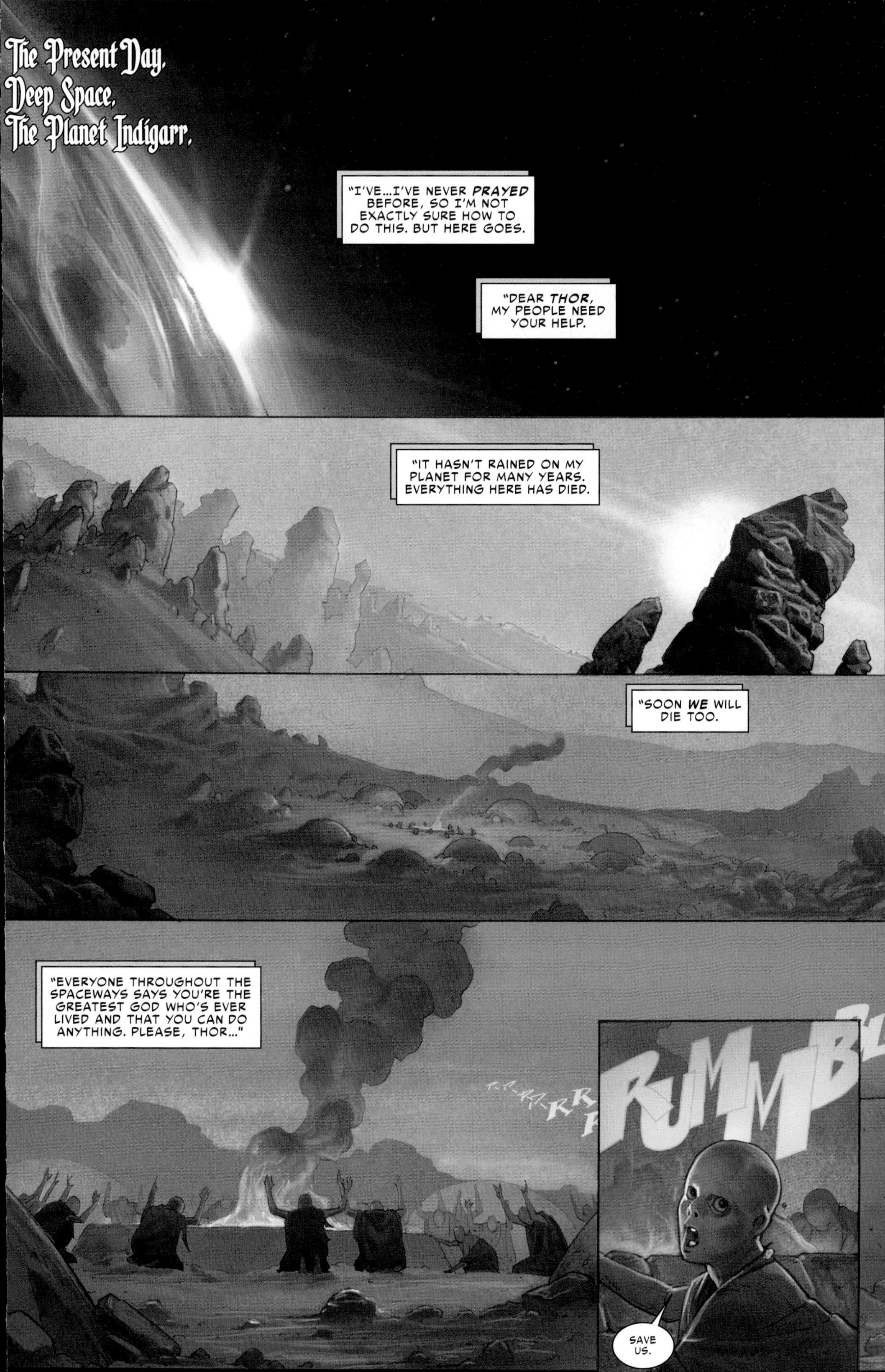
The Present Day, Deep Space, The Planet Indigarr,
"I'VE...I'VE NEVER PRAYED BEFORE, SO I'M NOT EXACTLY SURE HOW TO DO THIS. BUT HERE GOES.
"DEAR THOR, MY PEOPLE NEED YOUR HELP.
"IT HASN'T RAINED ON MY PLANET FOR MANY YEARS. EVERYTHING HERE HAS DIED.
"SOON WE WILL DIE TOO.
"EVERYONE THROUGHOUT THE SPACEWAYS SAYS YOU'RE THE GREATEST GOD WHO'S EVER LIVED AND THAT YOU CAN DO ANYTHING. PLEASE, THOR..."
RUMMB
SAVE US.

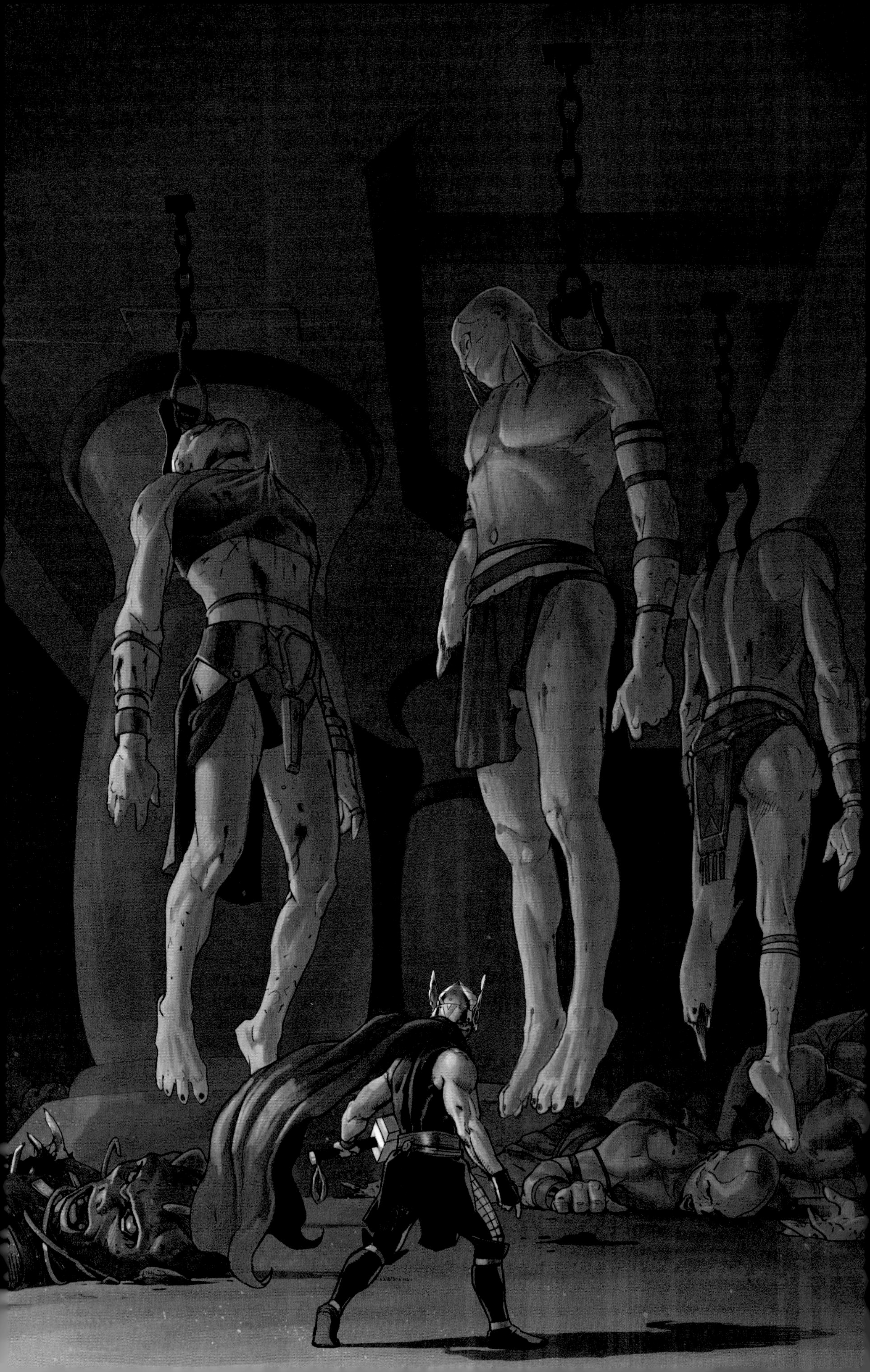

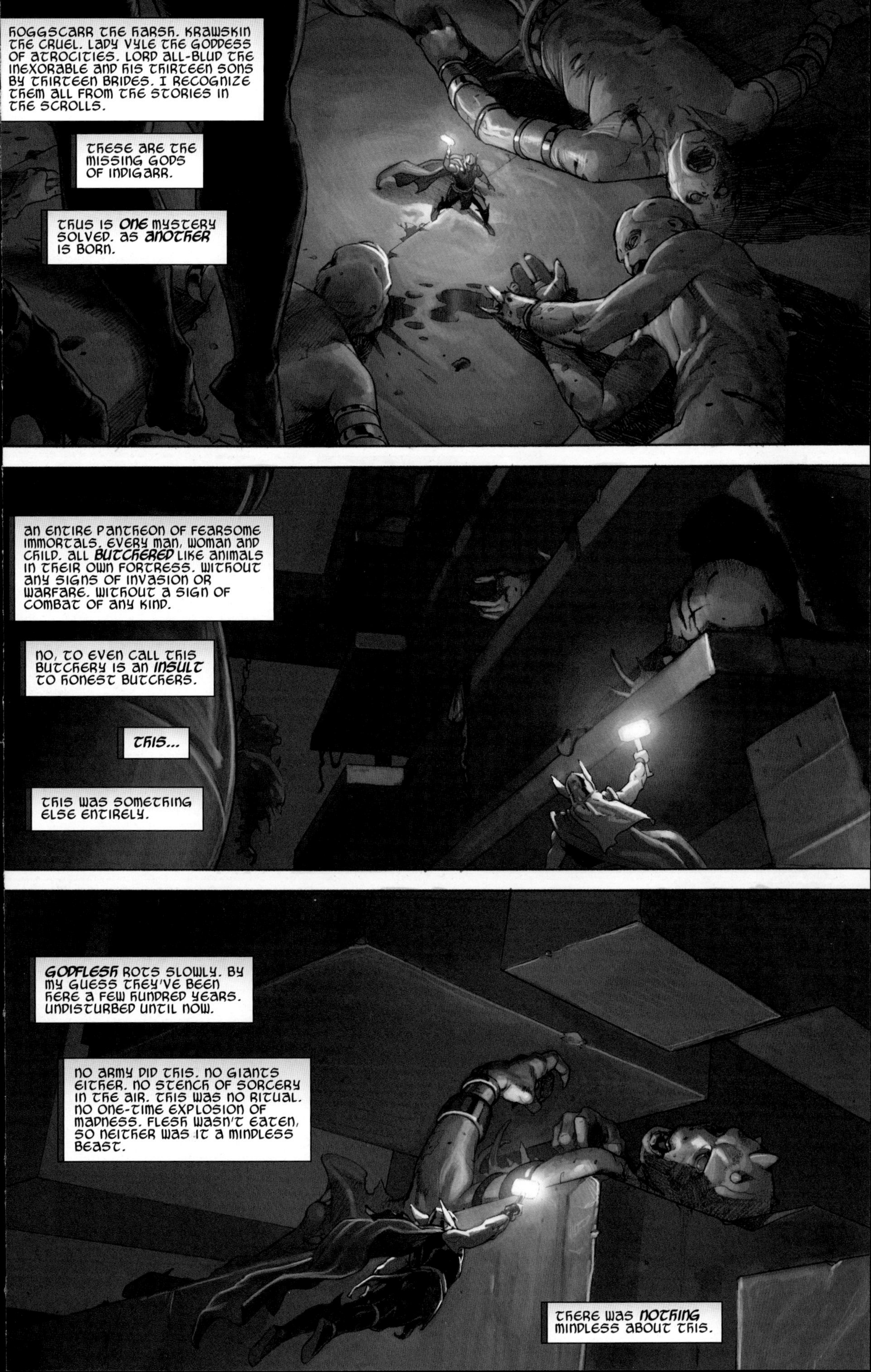
HOGGSCARR THE HARSH. KRAWSKIN THE CRUEL. LADY VYLE THE GODDESS OF ATROCITIES. LORD ALL-BLUD THE INEXORABLE AND HIS THIRTEEN SONS BY THIRTEEN BRIDES. I RECOGNIZE THEM ALL FROM THE STORIES IN THE SCROLLS.
THESE ARE THE MISSING GODS OF INDIGARR.
THUS IS ONE MYSTERY SOLVED. AS ANOTHER IS BORN.
AN ENTIRE PANTHEON OF FEARSOME IMMORTALS. EVERY MAN, WOMAN AND CHILD. ALL BUTCHERED LIKE ANIMALS IN THEIR OWN FORTRESS. WITHOUT ANY SIGNS OF INVASION OR WARFARE. WITHOUT A SIGN OF COMBAT OF ANY KIND.
NO, TO EVEN CALL THIS BUTCHERY IS AN INSULT TO HONEST BUTCHERS.
THIS...
THIS WAS SOMETHING ELSE ENTIRELY.
GODFLESH ROTS SLOWLY. BY MY GUESS THEY'VE BEEN HERE A FEW HUNDRED YEARS. UNDISTURBED UNTIL NOW.
NO ARMY DID THIS. NO GIANTS EITHER. NO STENCH OF SORCERY IN THE AIR. THIS WAS NO RITUAL. NO ONE-TIME EXPLOSION OF MADNESS. FLESH WASN'T EATEN, SO NEITHER WAS IT A MINDLESS BEAST.
THERE WAS NOTHING MINDLESS ABOUT THIS.

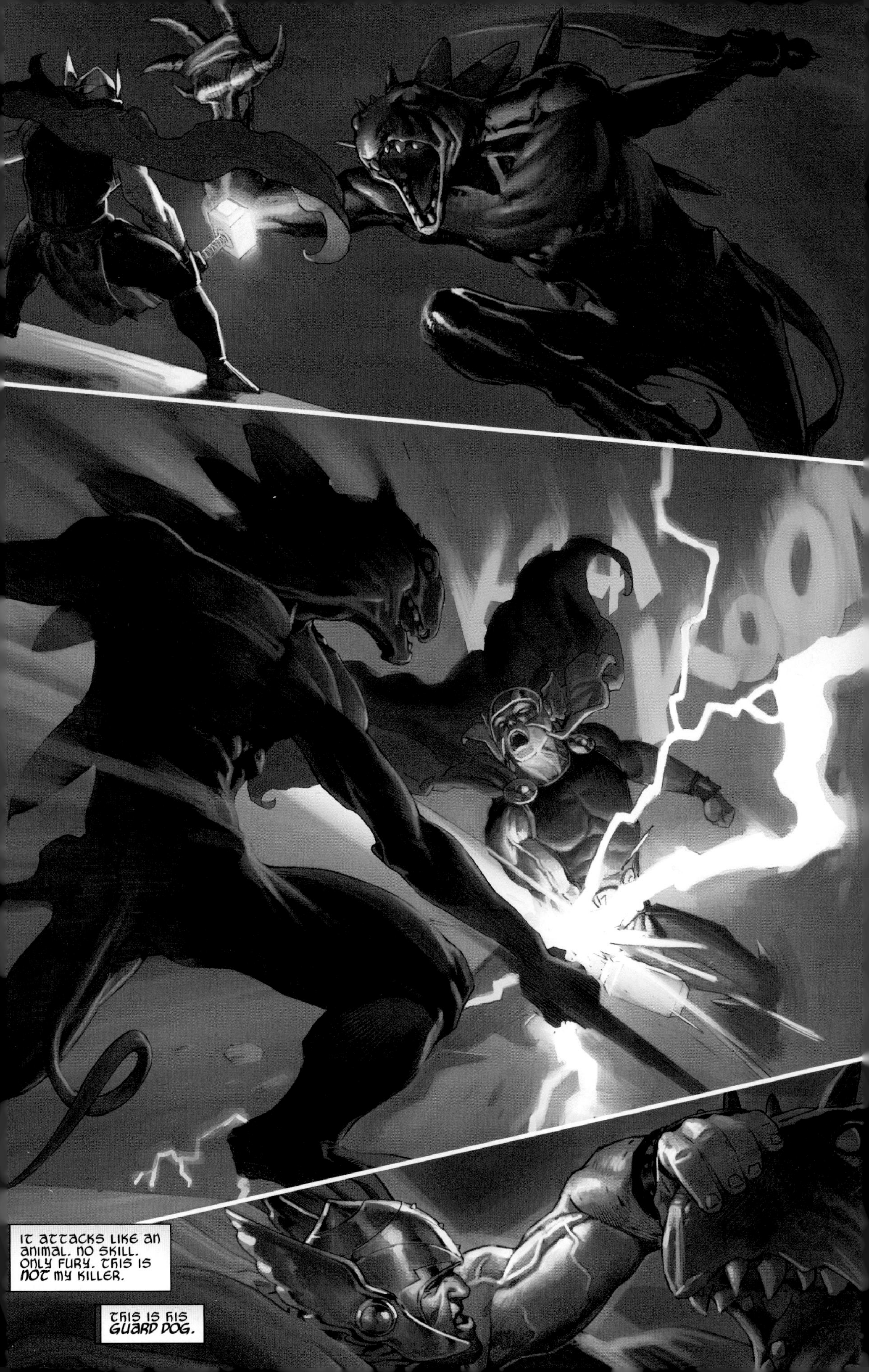
IT ATTACKS LIKE AN ANIMAL. NO SKILL. ONLY FURY. THIS IS *NOT* MY KILLER.
THIS IS HIS *GUARD DOG.*

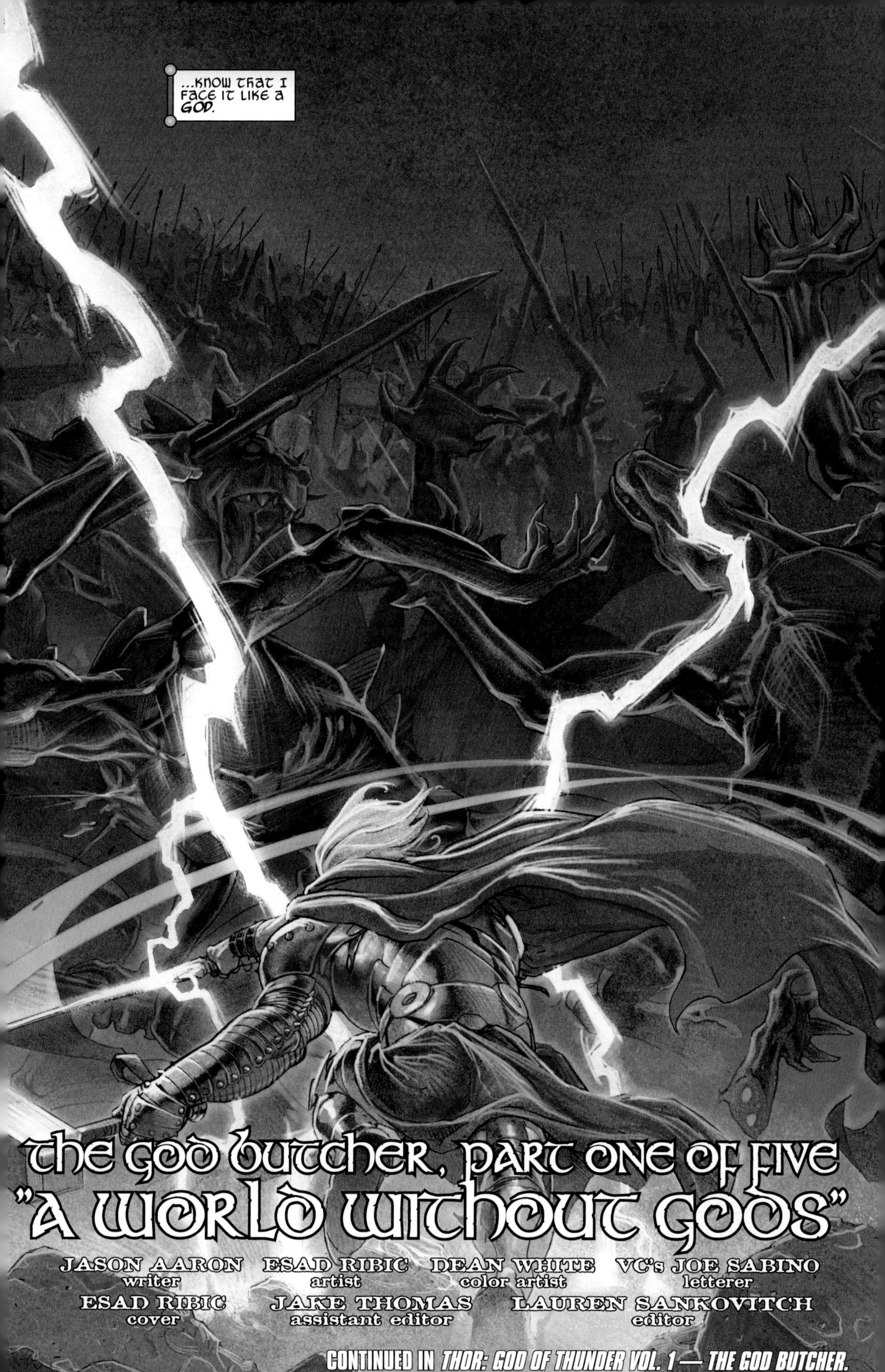
...KNOW THAT I FACE IT LIKE A GOD.
THE GOD BUTCHER, PART ONE OF FIVE
"A WORLD WITHOUT GODS"
JASON AARON writer
ESAD RIBIC artist
DEAN WHITE color artist
VC's JOE SABINO letterer
ESAD RIBIC cover
JAKE THOMAS assistant editor
LAUREN SANKOVITCH editor

CONTINUED IN *THOR: GOD OF THUNDER VOL. 1 — THE GOD BUTCHER.*

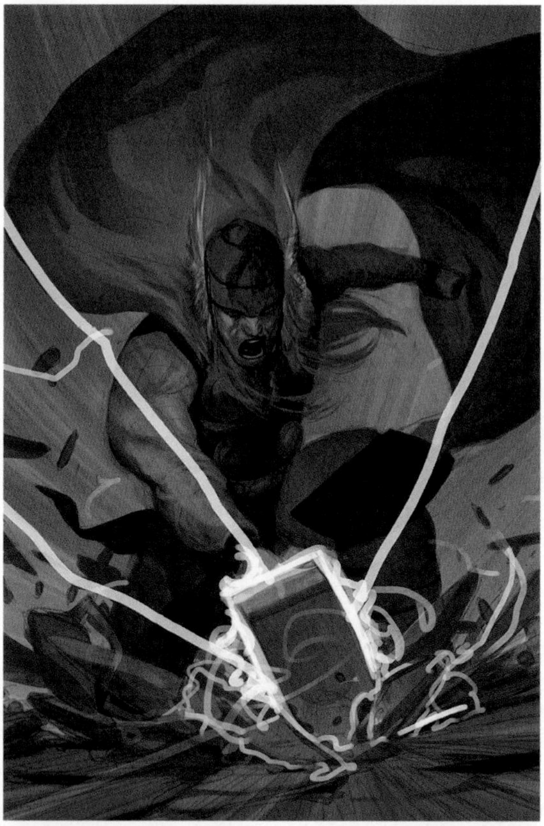

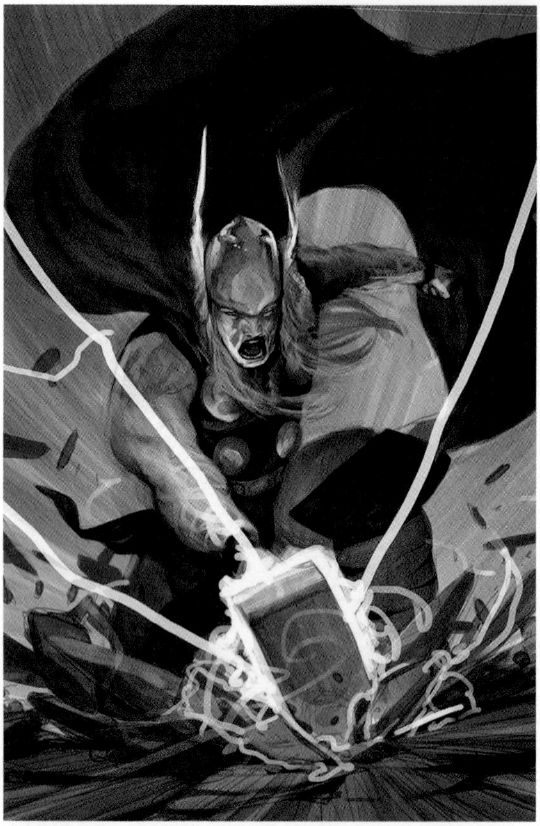

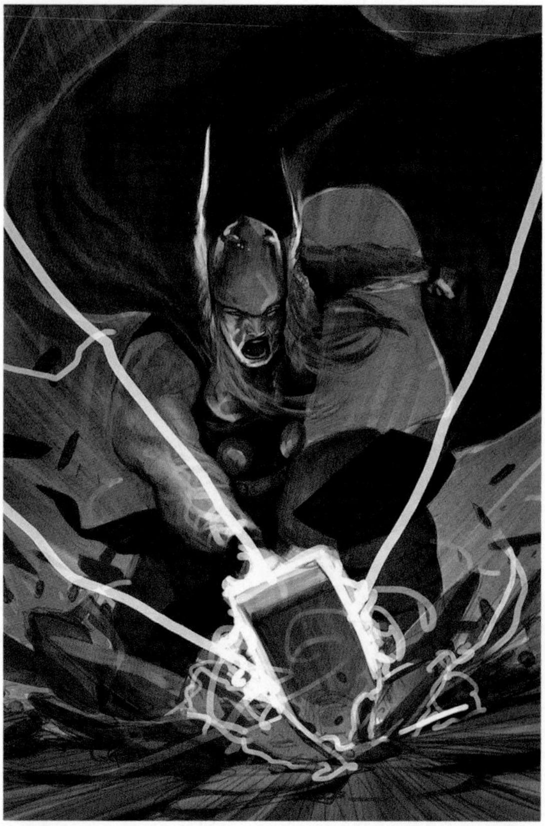

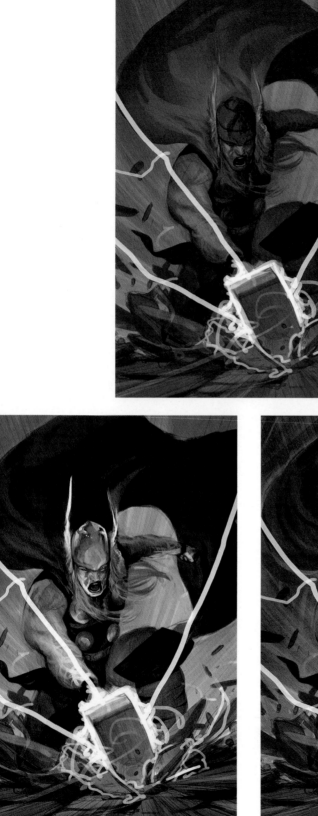

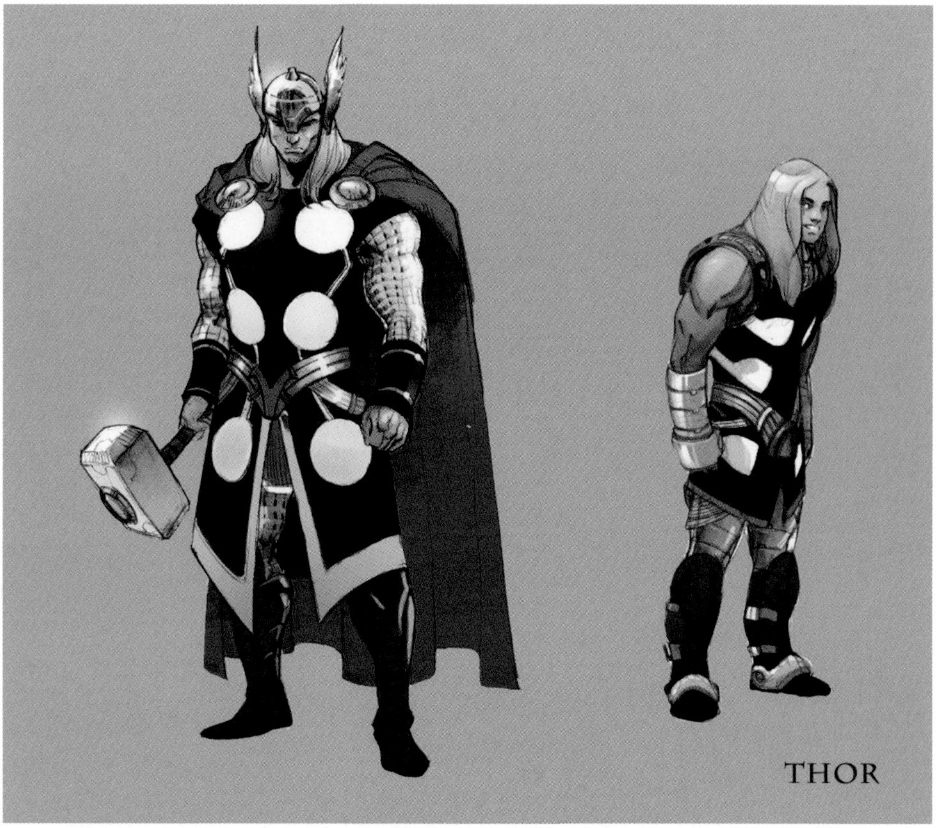
THOR

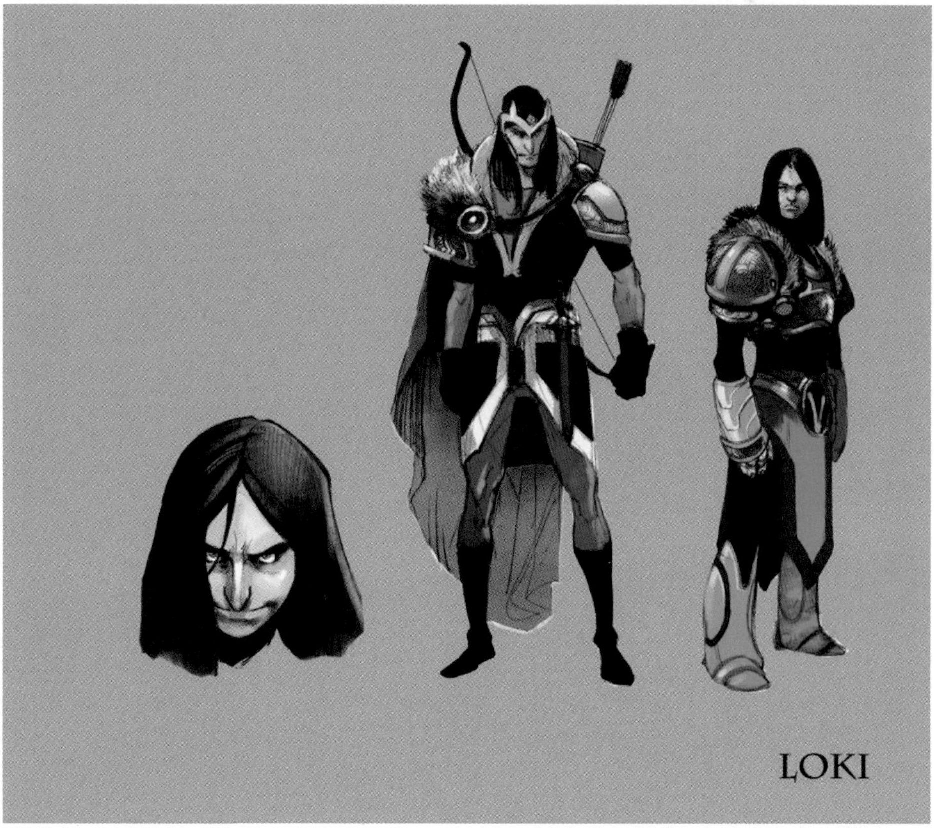
LOKI

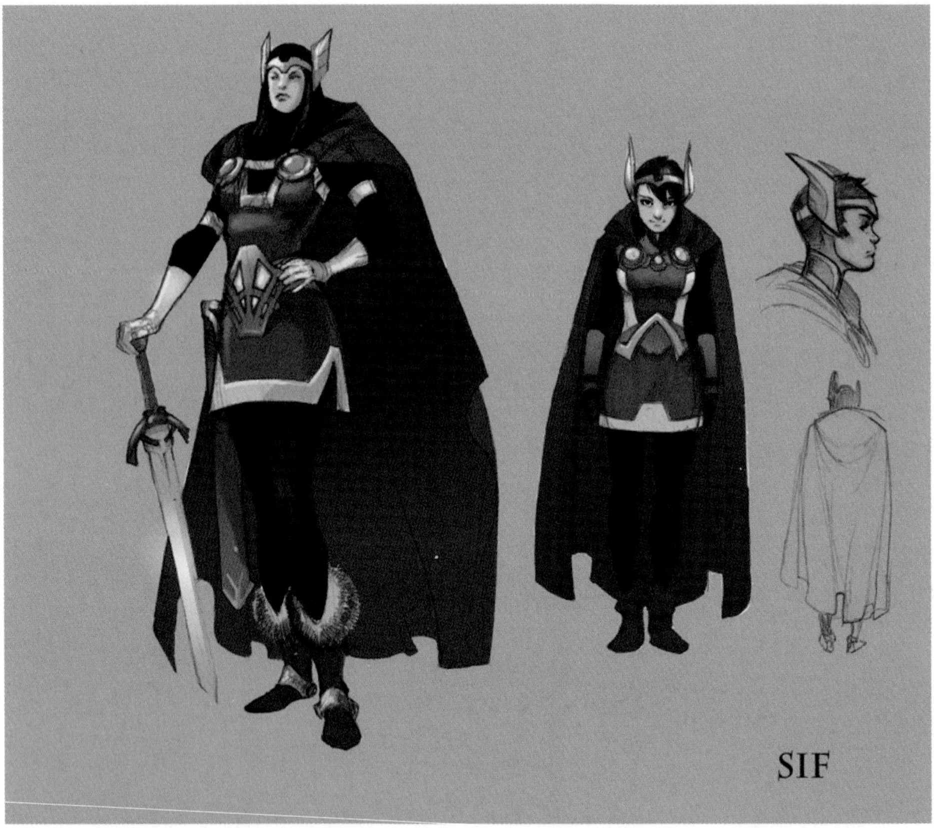
SIF

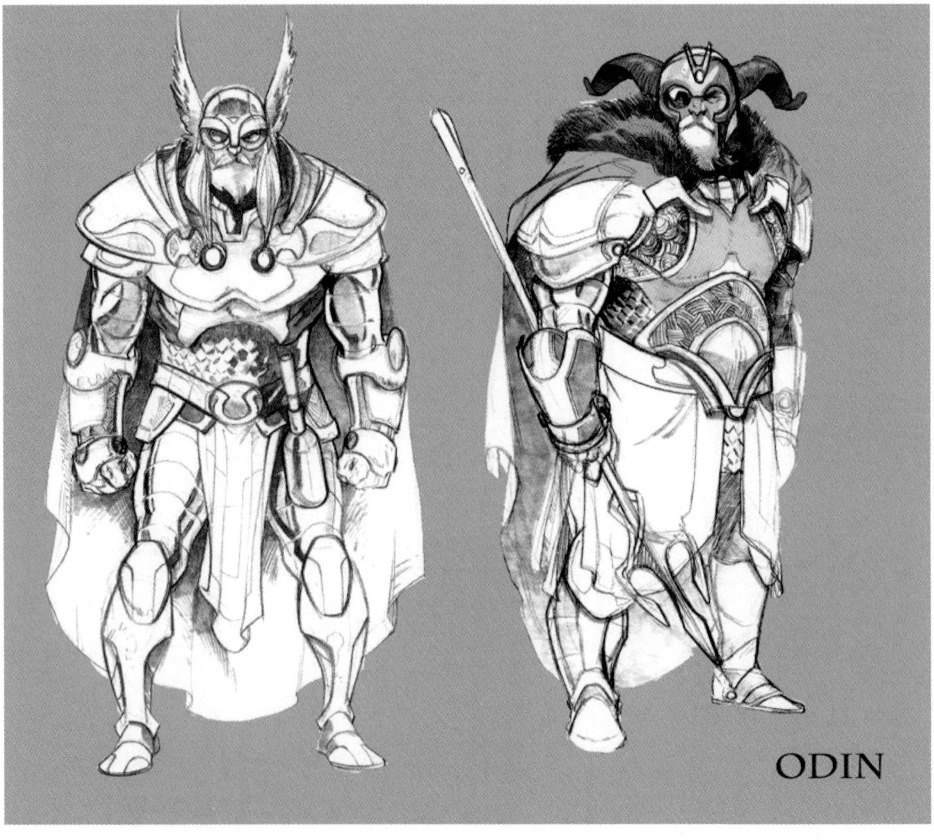
ODIN

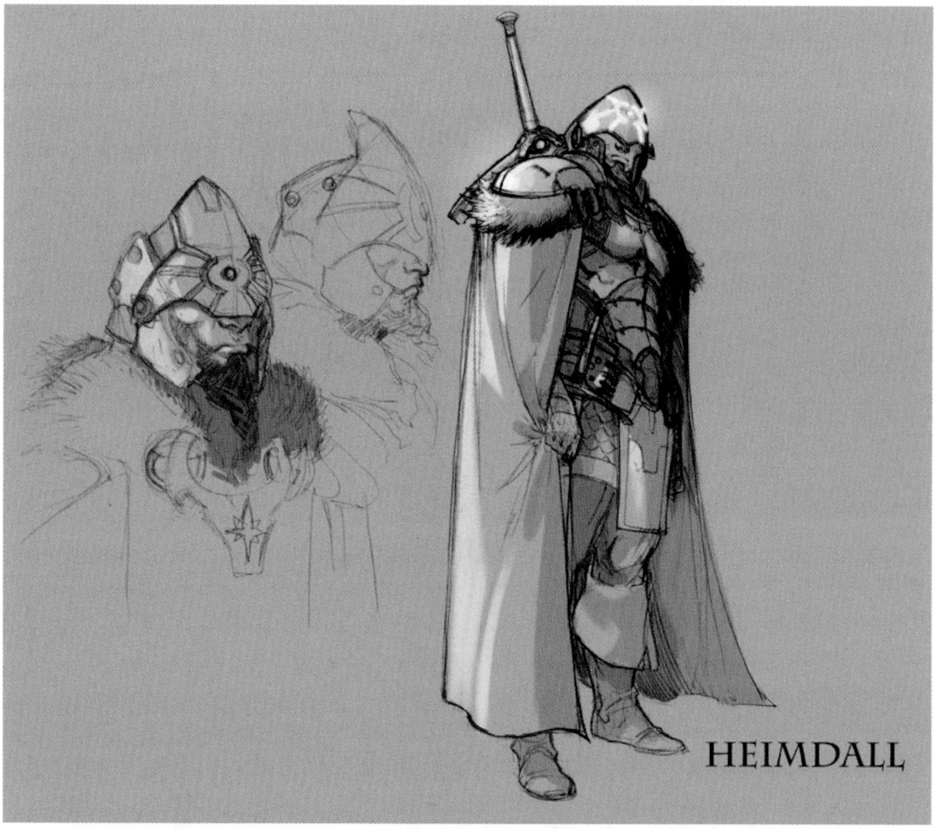
HEIMDALL

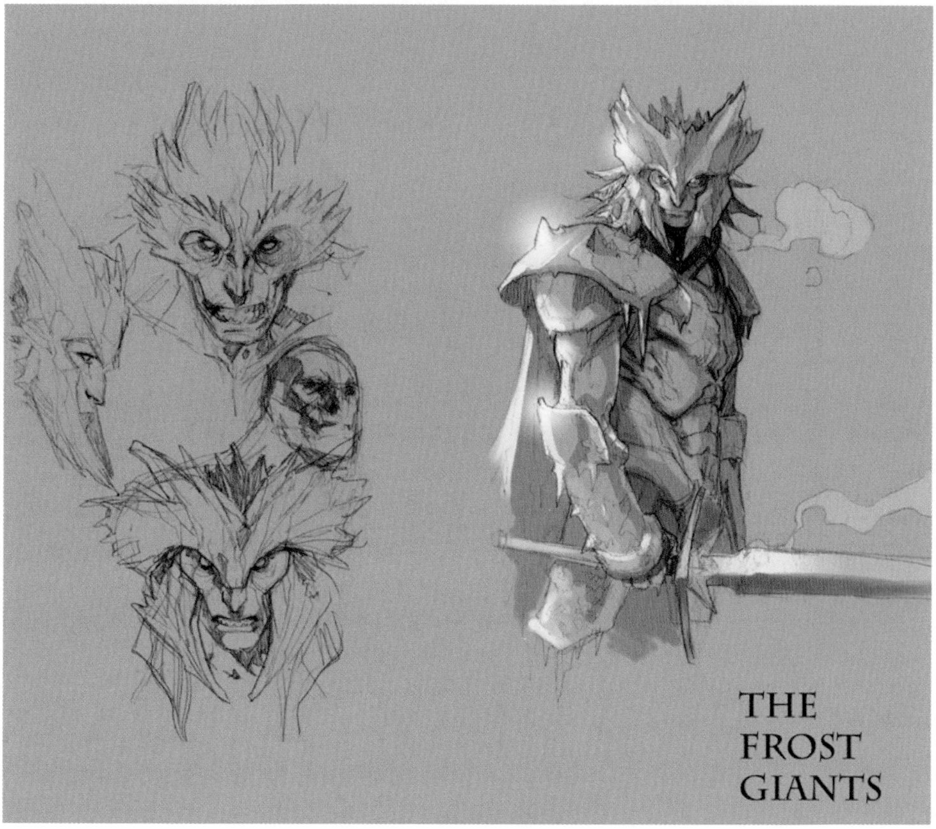
THE FROST GIANTS

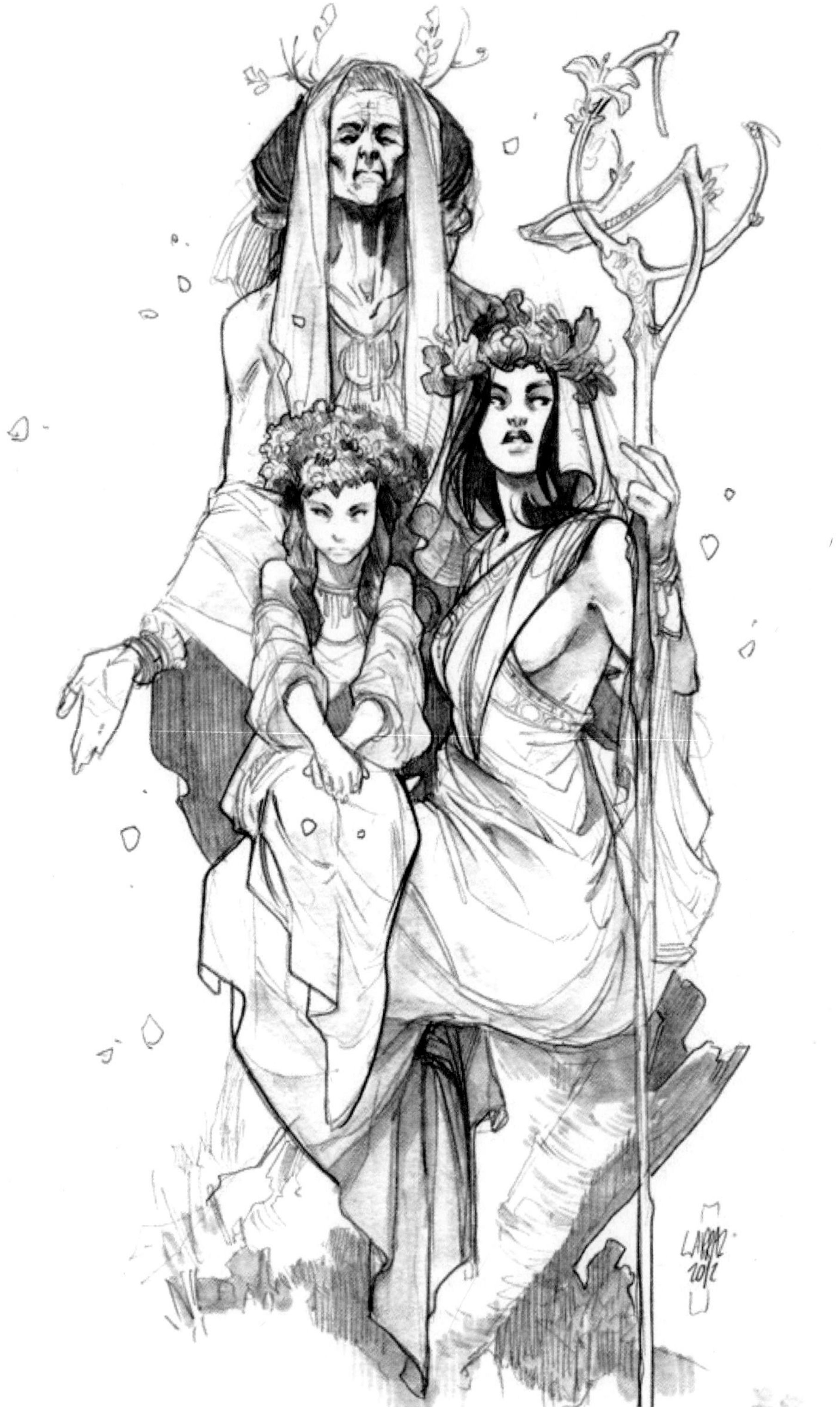

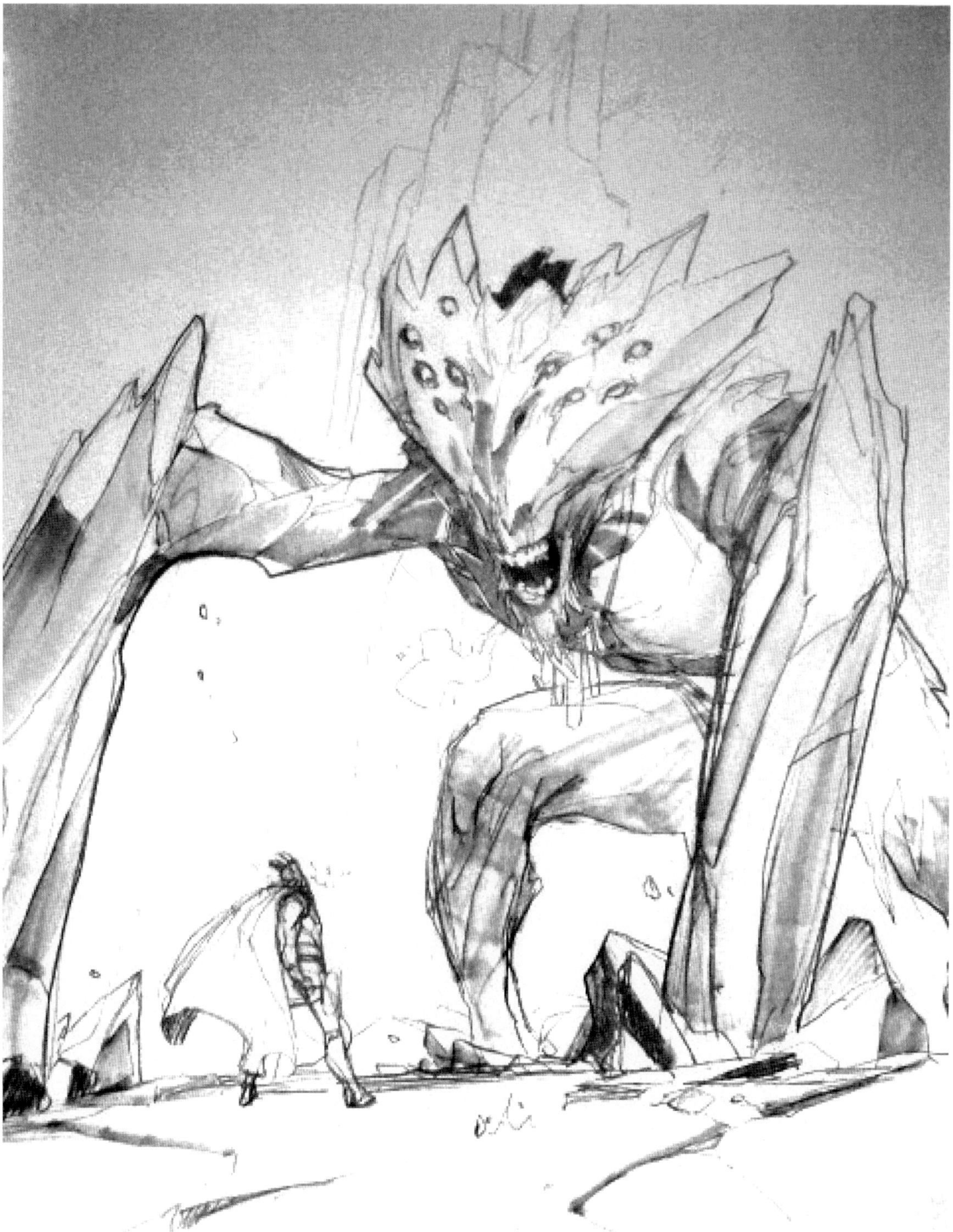

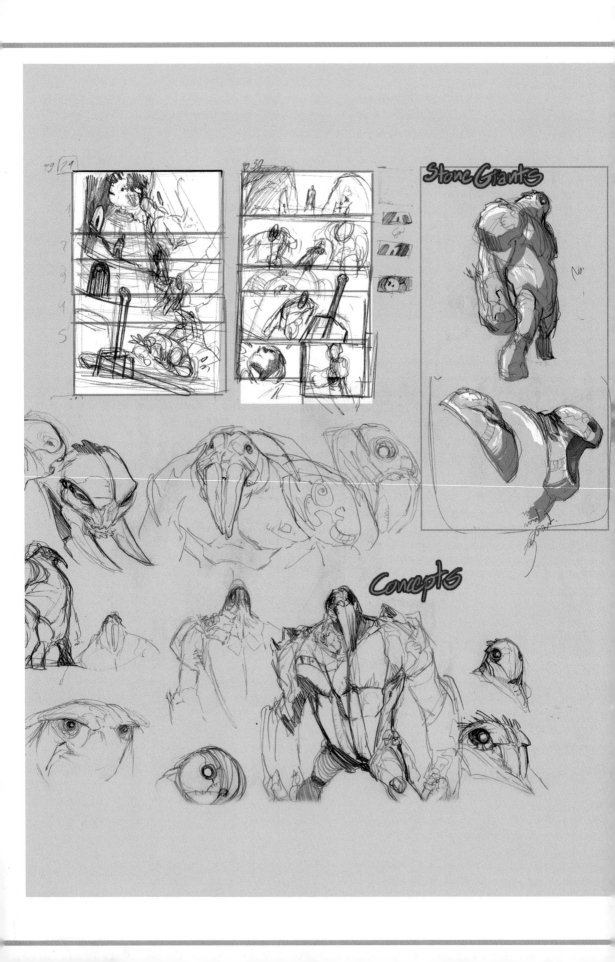

Stone Giants

Concepts

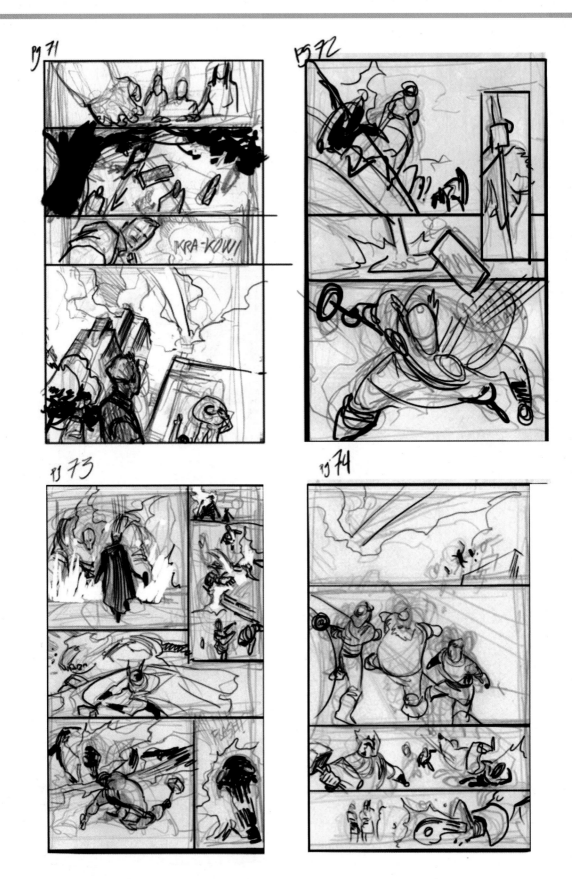

MARVEL

SEASON ONE

TOM DEFALCO • HORACIO DOMINGUES
ANT-MAN
MARVEL
SEASON ONE

ISBN # 978-0-7851-6386-2

GREG PAK • EMMA RIOS
DOCTOR STRANGE
MARVEL
SEASON ONE

ISBN # 978-0-7851-6388-6

FRED VAN LENTE • TOM FOWLER
HULK
MARVEL
SEASON ONE

ISBN # 978-0-7851-6387-9

DAVID • DI VITO • BURAN • RAYNOR • BOWDEN
AVENGERS
BONUS
DIGITAL EDITION
included
MARVEL
SEASON ONE

ISBN # 978-0-7851-6596-5

AVAILABLE WHEREVER BOOKS ARE SOLD.

MARVEL

Available Now In All Comic Shops & The Marvel Comics App
Comic Shop Locator: comicshoplocator.com
Marvel Comics App : marvel.com/marvelcomicsapp

MARVEL

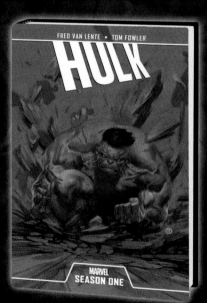